I d a K a r

PHOTOGRAPHER

1908 - 1974

Val Williams

VIRAGO

This book is dedicated to Frances Williams
and to Meg, who grew as it grew.

Published by VIRAGO PRESS Limited 1989
20–23 Mandela Street, Camden Town, London NW1 0HQ

Copyright © Val Williams 1989

All rights reserved

Design by Lone Morton

Published with financial assistance from the Arts Council
and the Andrew Sproxton Memorial Fund

A CIP record for this title is available from
the British Library

Printed in Great Britain by
Butler & Tanner Ltd
Frome and London

CONTENTS

7 ACKNOWLEDGEMENTS

INTRODUCTION   9   **Pictures of the lost decade**
An introduction to Ida Kar's photography

CHAPTER ONE   11   **Becoming Idabel**
From Armenia to Alexandra 1908–1945

CHAPTER TWO   16   **I looked in from the outside, and what did I see?**
Photographing bohemia in the 1950s

CHAPTER THREE   35   **In this purblind land**
Photography in the 1950s and the Whitechapel exhibition

CHAPTER FOUR   49   **Inheriting the party**
Life and work from 1960 to 1974

156   APPENDIX

157   NOTES

ACKNOWLEDGEMENTS

I acknowledge with gratitude the assistance of those who have searched their memories or their archives to give me information about, or impressions of, the life and work of Ida Kar.

Without the help of John Couzins, Mark Gerson, Julieta Green (formerly Preston), Josef Herman, Bill Hopkins, Heinrich Heidersberger, John Kasmin and John Morris, this account would have been seriously lacking.

After Ida Kar's death in 1974, her papers and photographs were collected together by Victor Musgrave and Mark Gerson. This archive has now passed to the stewardship of Monika Kinley, and I am indebted to her for her continuous assistance and friendship and for giving me access to all the papers and photographs associated with Ida's career and with her personal life.

Special thanks are due to Dorothy Bohm, who translated material from the original German, and has provided me with important papers about Ida's career. Amanda Hopkinson made skilled translations from the French of Ida's early letters from Egypt.

To all those who responded to my letters and enquiries about Ida, I am most grateful: Ernie Baker; Sandra Blow; Jane Bown; Lynn Chadwick; Bryn Campbell; Geoffrey Crawley (*British Journal of Photography*); Shelagh Delaney; Daniel Farson; Dame Elisabeth Frink; Lady Antonia Fraser; Terry Frost; Penelope Gilliatt; William Gear; Helmut Gernsheim; Patrick Heron; the late Stanley Hayter; Mark Haworth-Booth (Victoria and Albert Museum); Carol Hogben; Chris Killip; Robert Lassam (Fox Talbot Museum); Doris Lessing; Alan Osborne; Terence Pepper; Natalie Preston; Myfanwy and John Piper; Colette Soulages; Jack Smith; William Scott; F. N. Souza and Colin Wilson.

Charlotte Sankey of the *British Journal of Photography* made available to me the 1950s and 1960s volumes of the *Journal*. Grace Robertson and Godfrey Thurston Hopkins gave me many valuable insights into the state of photography in Britain in the 1950s. My thanks also to *Creative Camera* magazine, which published an appeal for information about Ida's career. The staff of the Photographers Gallery, London, especially Sue Davies and Zelda Cheatle, were as helpful as ever.

My thanks to Paul Evans, and to Florrie and Joe Evans for all their help, and to Phyllis Antonis for continuous support.

Thanks also to Ruthie Petrie and Melanie Silgardo at Virago, and to the Arts Council of Great Britain and the Andrew Sproxton Memorial Fund for their financial assistance.

Unless stated otherwise, all the photographs printed in this book are from the Ida Kar Archive and are reproduced by kind permission of Monika Kinley.

Valuable additional biographical illustrations were made available to the author by Anthony Gross, and his generosity regarding this material is gratefully acknowledged.

'Almost anything can be an art ... the making of shoes,
the planting of a garden, the designing of furniture,
just so long as the person who does it is himself an artist'

From an interview with Ida Kar in the *British Journal of Photography*,
16 March 1962

Pictures of the lost decade

An introduction to Ida Kar's photography

'Photography is above all reporting *and forming. There is, after all, only a difference in degree, no absolute distinction.'*[1]

Self portrait, 1955, used on the cover of Ida's 1960 Whitechapel exhibition catalogue

Ida Kar is a striking figure within the history of photography. Her work, and the attention which it received from press and public, heralded the beginning of the post-war photographic revival in Britain. Her exhibition at the Whitechapel Art Gallery in 1960 persuaded both establishment and artists that photography no longer needed to be confined to the pages of picture magazines or relegated to family record. If any one person might be said to have re-established photography as a respected art form in post-war London, then that distinction must go to Ida Kar.

Ida Kar took British portrait photography away from the whimsy and elegance which had so distinguished it in the twenties and early thirties. She replaced style with documentary, and produced a record of English bohemia which equals in perspicacity those of her eminent contemporaries John Deakin, Cecil Beaton and Douglas Glass. From her contemporaries, she is marked out by her intense interest in the humanity of her subjects. She was fascinated by their sexuality, by their ways of sitting and standing, by their obsessions and their vanities. With her half-innocent, half-knowing eye, she peered through her lens and penetrated the surface of the 1950s and gazed at the conflicts and the anxieties which characterised the decade. Difficult as she sometimes found the post-war years, when interest in her work was almost non-existent and support for her photographic projects confined to only a few loyal friends, it was hardly likely, with her vitality and optimism, that she would have agreed with Kenneth Allsop's judgment of the 1950s as a time of 'fearful stagnation'.[2] More likely it was that she shared in the excitement of the years which produced Beckett's *Waiting for Godot* (first seen in London in 1955), Colin Wilson's revolutionary treatise *The Outsider* (in 1956), Jackson Pollock's exhibition at the Whitechapel (in 1958) and Brendan Behan's fiery 1958 play, *The Hostage*.

When Ida Kar conducted a portrait session, she was as much a reporter as a maker of likenesses. When she photographed the young novelist Iris Murdoch (page 90) kneeling among pages of manuscript, it is as if she is intruding on some intense moment of concentration. There is a sense of conflict between portrayer and portrayed. When she photographed Laurie Lee (page 118) loose-lipped against a background of pin-ups, she gently explores ideas of lust and lasciviousness. More than any other photographer working in Britain since the Second World War, Ida Kar evoked the spirit of her times. She portrayed a peculiarly English bohemia, situated in London's Soho, and closely observed a tentative and somewhat weary avant garde. She paid particular attention to settings and situations, and her use of the artist's studio is one which she returned to time and again to convey the singularly claustrophobic nature of British creativity. She portrayed artists in their own settings, and acutely juxtaposed maker with object, making continuous connections between the process and the producer. In her portraits of, for instance, Lynn Chadwick (page 99) and Kenneth Armitage one can almost feel the transference of power between the sculptor and the sculpture; both men sit at rest, their power transferred to the object before them.

Compared with earlier practitioners Ida Kar took British portrait photography away from notions of sycophancy and celebrity. She ensured that the portraitist no longer needed to be the publicist. The joy of her photography lies in her almost faultless description of the main characters of post-war British cultural life. She portrays a society which has disappeared – the British art world in its post-war innocence, a civilisation in limbo, a heavenly demi-paradise of bohemia due to disappear for ever as the economic and social climate changed.

The coffee bars and the shabby artists' studios of Soho have long gone, and Ida Kar's enormous presence, her resonant tones and her astonishing ability to override convention are now simply memories. But her photographs remain, to testify to the peculiar ambiguities of the 1950s, that strangely lost decade which combined so much of arrogance and innocence, of generosity and cruelty, of anger and apathy.

Kenneth Armitage, sculptor, 1954

CHAPTER ONE

Becoming Idabel
From Armenia to Alexandria 1908–1945

'We travelled as a matter or course. I rejoice that I went when the going was good.'[1]

Ida, aged about two years, c. 1910 (*Private collection*)

Ida Karamian was born in Tambov in the USSR in 1908. Her early years were spent in Russia, in Iran and, from the age of thirteen, in Egypt. The Karamians settled in Alexandria, where Ida's father Melkon pursued his teaching career, and Ida continued her education at the Lycée Francais in Alexandria. Melkon Karamian was determined that his only daughter should have a career, and in 1928, encouraged her to travel to Paris, to take up studies in medicine and chemistry. What kind of a physician Ida Kar would have been remains a matter of conjecture, for she had soon abandoned her studies in favour of an intense course of lessons in singing and the violin, and was living and working among the young avant garde of the Left Bank.

Ida's music studies led to an important friendship. She became acquainted with Suzanne Dumesnil, a progressive woman and skilled musician, later to become the companion and wife of Samuel Beckett. At Dumesnil's home in the thirteenth arrondissement, Ida met a young German surrealist painter and photographer, Heinrich Heidersberger. To Heidersberger, the twenty-two year old Ida was a striking figure, dark-haired and dark-eyed – exotic. She seemed to him to be 'a young girl, almost a teenager'[2] and their friendship grew and prospered as the 1920s drew to a close.

Ida had arrived in Paris when the city was at its most excitingly international, and when its position as centre of the arts was unrivalled. Some six years before Ida's arrival from Alexandria, the young American Sylvia Beach had published (in 1922) the first edition of James Joyce's *Ulyssees*, and by the late twenties, the best of European and American writing and painting was available to all through the medium of adventurous small magazines. Eugene Jolas's periodical, *Transition* was only one way in which new Paris residents might see the work of artists like Man Ray, Kurt Schwitters and Max Ernst. Huge innovations were taking place throughout the

Family gathering in Armenia, c. 1914. (*Private collection*)

Growing up in Alexandria: Ida (right) and a friend, early 1920s

arts. Audiences had given an enthusiastic reception to Luis Buñuel's film *Un Chien Andalous*, and both Ida and Heinrich Heidersberger had been present for its first showing at the house of the Surrealist group in Studio 20 at the rue du Chateau.

It was in Paris in the late twenties that Ida first became aware of the potential of photography. After their initial meeting, a friendship of strength and intensity grew between Ida and Heinrich Heidersberger, and eventually, they became lovers, sharing an apartment on the rue Perrier in Montrouge. Heidersberger had 'begun to make reproductions with a wooden camera bought at the fleamarket'[3], and, with Ida looking on, he 'exposed the plates to the moonlight which entered through the glass roof', and then made contact prints.[4] Ida herself recalled, many years later, that she first became intrigued by photography when she acted as a model for Heidersberger during these first experiments. Together, they visited photo exhibitions, and could not have failed to be aware of the new modernism in photography emanating from Germany, and enthusiastically received in Paris. Seminal German books like Karl Blossfeldt's *Urformen der Kunst* (1928) and Werner Graff's *Es Kommt der Neue Fotograf* (1929) were readily available to Parisian enthusiasts. By the time that Ida had arrived in the city, André Kertész had already held his first one-man show at the Sacre du Printemps Gallery (in 1927), and Berenice Abbott had shown her influential *Portraits Photographiques*. In 1926, the future photo-documentarist Walker Evans arrived in Paris from the United States for a year's study at the Sorbonne, and at *Vogue* magazine, Lucien Vogel was influencing a whole generation of young photographers. At the very centre of photographic activity was Man Ray, the pioneering experimentalist who had made his first Rayogram in Paris in 1922, and who numbered among his students in the twenties Berenice Abbott and the British photographer Bill Brandt. Also in Paris from the mid-1920s were Paul Outerbridge, Horst P. Horst, George Hoyningen-Huene, and, from 1929, the documentarist Brassai, whose seminal study of Parisian street life, *Paris by Night* was published in 1933.

Undoubtedly Ida's interest in photography was stimulated in these early years in France. Frequent visits to art galleries, bookshops and the cinema gave her important insights into European cultural initiatives. She attended a showing of Eisenstein's *Battleship Potemkin* (projected in an attic) and Heinrich Heidersberger remembers the thrill of the occasion: 'The screen was moving in the draught, so that the red coloured flag appeared to move on the screen in a special rhythm when it was projected in

In Alexandria in the early 1930s. Ida is the young woman at the centre of the photograph, with her mother and father on either side. (*Private collection*)

Ida, aged twenty-six, Alexandria, 1934

the final shot. It was as though we were part of a conspiracy in that room.'[5]

Even in those early years, Ida was fascinated and intrigued by the lives of writers and artists, and through Heidersberger, she met many important innovators, and, for the first time, encountered the orderly jumble of the artist's studio, laying the foundations for a fascination with the patterning and surfaces of painting and sculpture workshops which was to direct and inform much of her later work in photography. A particular friendship developed with the Dutch artist Gerard Hordyk, and his American wife Margaret,[6] and Piet Mondrian and Yves Tanguy were members of the group of people with whom Ida and Heidersberger mixed. A favourite diversion for Ida was to visit the small dance bars used by artists, and with Heidersberger she attended some of the large artists' parties which were a feature of Parisian life at the end of the twenties.

The Paris years also saw Ida's growing interest in politics: 'she was a totally committed revolutionary, politically left wing just as everyone in artistic circles was at the time of the surrealists.'[7] Ida's political convictions stayed with her for the remainder of her life, and during the 1960s, she became a loyal supporter of the Cuban revolution. (Sometimes, in later life, she would jot down thoughts on politics in her notebooks, and in the mid-1960s, offered to contribute photographs free of charge to Labour's *Tribune* newspaper.)

By the end of 1933, Ida had returned to Alexandria, taking with her a keepsake from Heidersberger: 'a small work which I entitled "Charlie Chaplin", and which was a kind of "assemblage" made up of all sorts of material and a montage of these.'[8] During her four years in France, she had acquired a sophisticated knowledge of European art, film-making and literature. Alexandria, in contrast to Paris, had little to offer her. She rejected the bourgeois life of her family and friends, but at the same time was unable to decide which direction her life should take. Acute problems with her voice prevented her from continuing with her singing career, and an unhappy love affair made her despair of ever regaining the happiness which she had found in Paris. After the freedoms of France, she found the moral strictures of middle-class Armenian society irksome. From her parents' home in the rue Tanis she wrote in 1934:

this existence has completely defeated me. My voice has been in need of special care, but I haven't had enough heart to look after myself. I've experienced a profound disgust for life. If I stay in this accursed country, I'll probably never love again ... My life

Studio portrait of Ida, late 1920s, Alexandria. (*Private collection*)

Ida with her dog in Alexandria, mid-1930s. (*Private collection*)

is very sad, and I'm spending the best years of my life like an old maid.[9]

Ida's liking for children led her to consider undertaking a course of training as a nursery nurse, and she considered the possibility of enrolling as a student at a kindergarten in Paris. It was, however, her unexpected involvement with photography which was to direct the course of future events, from the mid-1930s onwards. In later life, Ida was asked to recall the beginning of her interest in photography for the benefit of the critics who flocked to her Whitechapel exhibition in 1960. Although her own story of her early career was possibly a dramatised one, there was probably much truth in her account:

> She became a photographer as the direct result of losing her voice while studying singing in Paris. On her return to her native city, still undecided about the future, she happened, while walking through town, to stop in front of a photographic studio. The owner, who was at the moment standing in the doorway, asked her without more ado to become his assistant/receptionist, and Ida Kar impulsively agreed, on condition that she would be allowed to use the studio facilities during her free time.[10]

Like many other illustrious photographers of the twenties and thirties, Ida learned her craft by practising on her friends and relations. Soon, she began to meet others who were involved in the medium. One fellow enthusiast was Edmond Belali, an Egyptian government official and serious amateur photographer who became Ida's first husband. Married in the late thirties, the two photographers moved to Cairo, where they established a small studio, called after their joint names – *Idabel*. According to Ida's own accounts, the studio was uncompromisingly artistic, refusing to take 'conventional pictures, static wedding groups or frozen passports'.[11] The premises were decorated in modern style, and Ida would place a single long-stemmed flower in an elegant vase in the shop-window to deter the casual passer-by. Problems arose inevitably when 'Ida's ideas of what a good portrait should be differed so often from those of her clients that business was non-existent, and she had to take a variety of part-time jobs in order to keep going.'[12] Sadly, no photographs from Ida's pre-war years can now be traced, but those of her friends who have vague memories of her Egyptian work recall large moody close-ups and surrealistic still lifes.

Uncompromising or not, Idabel's sternly artistic approach to

Surreal study, London c. 1947

portraiture appears to have paid off. When the young Victor Musgrave, stationed in war-time Cairo and contributing pieces of art criticism to the *Egyptian Gazette*, encountered Ida Kar in the early forties, the studio was operating from a fashionable quarter of Cairo, and was much liked among the cosmopolitan set of writers and artists who congregated in the city during the war years. So well thought of was the work of *Idabel* that Ida and Belali were accepted as exhibitors in the two surrealist exhibitions staged in Cairo in 1943 and 1944 and the business prospered.

The arrival of Victor Musgrave, a young, talented and exceptionally charming Englishman, into Ida's life signalled the beginning of a relationship which was to endure, in pleasure and in pain, for the next two decades. During the war years, Ida divorced Edmond Belali, and in her thirty-sixth year, she and Victor were married, and living in 'their amazing home in the Darb el Labana [which] became the resort of artists and writers visiting Cairo from all over the world'.[13] From cosmopolitan Cairo, they were soon to set off on another adventure, to explore and to inhabit an entirely new bohemia.

CHAPTER TWO

I looked in from the outside, and what did I see?

Photographing bohemia in the 1950s

'For it is closing time in the gardens of the West, and from now on, an artist will be judged by the resonance of his solitude and the quality of his despair.'[1]

When Ida Kar and Victor Musgrave arrived in London in 1945, they encountered a culture in chaos. They had come from cosmopolitan Cairo, where their experiences had been crowned by their wedding, theatrically celebrated amid crowds of children, hundreds of balloons and a procession of entertainers, to a London which was impoverished, uncertain and bewildered. Like many of those who were returning at the War's end, they looked to bohemia for reassertion and regeneration.

By the time they had settled into a small flat in Devonshire Close, just around the corner from Regents Park, Ida was again immersed in her photography. Soon after she arrived in London, she had arranged with Olwen Vaughan to show some of her work at the New London Film Society, and in 1947, she was exhibiting alongside the sculptor Coturier at the Anglo-French Art Centre in St John's Wood. Victor continued to write, becoming a scriptwriter for Gainsborough Films in 1947, and by the end of the 1940s, Ida began to advertise as a theatrical photographer. The new life began in earnest, however, when Ida and Victor moved to a dilapidated building in Litchfield Street, just off the Charing Cross Road, where the painter John Christoforou had established a small gallery intended for the showing of his own work. Victor Musgrave was 'recruited by Christoforou to staff the exhibition space while he painted in his studio'[2] and even Ida at times left the small studio she had opened on one of the upper floors to open the gallery and show paintings to clients.

By 1953, Christoforou had left London for Paris and the South of France, leaving Victor and Ida as the guardians and tenants of the Litchfield Street rooms. Ramshackle as it was, with its missing floorboards and its rickety stairs, the building offered great possibilities. London's art galleries were beginning to revive and expand after the closures of the War. Young artists were emerging,

A portrait from the early 1950s. (*Private collection*)

John Christoforou, photographed by Ida at the house in Litchfield Street, 1953

and pre-war figures found themselves with no shortage of exhibition space and commissions. The 1951 Festival of Britain had caused a new confidence in British art, and the infant Arts Council of Great Britain had begun to organise large subsidised shows, illuminating particular aspects of British cultural achievement.

Litchfield Street itself was on the very edge of Soho, just a step away from the streets where artists and writers worked and met at Muriel Belcher's Colony Club or the York Minster pub, or at the Mandrake in Meard Street. David Archer's bookshop in Greek Street catered for avant garde tastes in literature; coffee bars multiplied, their potted palms and rough surfaced walls suggesting both aestheticism and exotica. To step through the looking glass out of austerity Britain and into bohemia was a necessary exercise for those who sought excitement, stimulation and opportunity in a city where such qualities were in short supply.

Ida was already a mature woman when she took up residence in Soho. She had lived in Armenia, Iran, Alexandria, Cairo and Paris, but even for someone of her experience, Soho became and remained both a place of stimulation and of security. In Soho she was, over the next ten years, to find her friends, her lovers and many of her photographic subjects. Many new friends came to visit Ida and Victor at Litchfield Street. The photographer Mark Gerson, who had established a studio in Marble Arch, had first met Ida when he rented darkroom space to her, and he soon became a regular visitor, remaining close to her until her death. 'There she was, this bizarre Armenian woman with a French accent, very flamboyant, she always dressed the part as well. All kinds of people were interested in her.'[3]

Mark Gerson was an early witness to Ida's photographic methods. Then and now, he judged her to be a photographer of great power, both as a creator of images and as a technician. Climbing the uneven stairs at Litchfield Street, he watched some of her portrait sittings:

> In the early days, she used an old plate camera. Her technique was a couple of photo-floods and bags of chat and then take the photograph. She'd talk about almost anything, usually their love life. People used to tell her things they wouldn't tell anyone else.[4]

The strength of Ida's personality quickly became apparent to those who befriended her in London. For Ida, who did not read, or take an interest in theatre or film, who travelled for business and rarely for pleasure, only people and photography were of interest. She was autocratic and demanding, but derived no pleasure from

Glamour among the ruins: Ida in London, late 1940s

manipulating or scandalising. She had no sense of irony and there was no room in her particular imagination for the subtleties of motive or discourse. Such forthrightness worked both for and against her, in her photography and in her life. In personal affairs, she became both victim and victimiser, exploiter and exploited. In her photographic career, while producing portraits which adhere to the first principles of fine photography – they do not flatter, they make a number of exact points about their subjects, they rise above notions of fashionability and eccentricity – she constantly misread the rules of the politics of success. For many of her sitters in the 1950s, Ida was bewildering and a little intimidating. Mark Gerson remembered well the effect that Ida could have on those she photographed: 'They loved it first of all, and then they got a bit frightened. Then of course they disappeared from her because she was too overwhelming. Everybody started off loving her and her personality, but they ended up saying, "My God, I can't stand any more of this".'[5]

Most of those who came to know Ida in Soho in the fifties suffered withdrawal symptoms at times, but some people, who came to love and respect her, rose above the fears and doubts which people like Ida most often bring about in the minds of those who are mindful of the precise boundaries of friendship. With Mark Gerson, Ida shared a common interest in the medium of photography. He was probably one of the few people she knew in London with whom she could discuss photographic matters, for although Ida made it her business to know exactly what other photographers were doing:

> She was always very jealous of other photographers, she'd say, 'They're no good.' She had to *know* what they were doing, but on the whole, she never thought a lot of them. . . . When I photographed Evelyn Waugh, she said, 'That really is quite good.' That was the greatest praise I ever got from her.[6]

Ida visited John Deakin's strong and idiosyncratic show of photographs taken in Paris, held at David Archer's bookshop in Greek Street in 1956, and also attended the first showing of Cartier Bresson's photographs in London, at the Institute of Contemporary Arts in 1952, and at different times in her career, she corresponded with both Cecil Beaton and the portraitist Douglas Glass. Generally though, her photographic preoccupations were centred upon herself and her own career and within the medium. While she could relate well to younger and more inexperienced photographers and to amateur groupings to whom she would give lectures as the fifties progressed, she had an instinctive distaste (or fear) for those who had progressed as far, or further than herself. Such tactics served only to isolate Ida from her peers in a practice which was already standing in dire isolation from the mainstream of the visual arts. The artist Josef Herman, to whom she remained close during the fifties, he posing for her, she for him, remembered that 'she didn't talk much about photography, she lived in her own world. From such a personality, you couldn't expect much objectivity. She *couldn't* get out of her skin, because her skin was so big'.

For Ida, at the beginning of the 1950s, life in Soho was a rich mixture of working, socialising, entertaining, cooking and conversation. For her, Soho and the people she knew there *were* London. The rest of the metropolis hardly existed, the remainder of Britain had no place in her consciousness, except when she had to travel to photograph an artist or writer who lived out of town. She knew all the market traders in Berwick Street, and became close friends with a group of elderly French prostitutes.[8] Many of her friends were Armenian or Jewish (often living in Britain as former refugees from Nazi Europe). An outsider herself, she felt most at ease with others who, because of nationality or race, were also strangers in a strange land.

Artists and writers visited Ida and Victor at Litchfield Street (and later, a few streets away, at D'Arblay Street), to be intrigued by Victor's charm and intellectualism, to be entertained by Ida's conversation ('she was always talking, at the top of her voice')[9], by her renderings of operatic arias and Armenian folk songs in her strong deep contralto, which had once been professionally trained in Paris. Ida always cooked for her guests, isolating herself in her tiny kitchen making meals whose ingredients and precise recipes were surrounded by mystery. The painter Josef Herman would make a point of visiting Ida whenever he was in London:

> She was such an endearing person, she was the quintessence of friendliness. She was a *real* friend, not just an unreliable ally. There were numbers of people who didn't have enough money or enough to eat, and she would feed them. She was an excellent cook, and when she was cooking, the whole world disappeared. There were meals to which you couldn't attach a name, because they were all very personal works, almost of art.[10]

Sometimes, visitors would prolong their stays, either because they had nowhere else to go, or when they became lodgers, by bringing much-needed funds into the household. The writers Bill Hopkins and Colin MacInnes both boarded with Ida and Victor at different

Josef Herman, painter, London, 1960

times during the fifties. Occasionally people came to stay because they had some other service to offer; the artist and jazz musician Sam Kramer was put up at Litchfield Street while he painted a mural for Ida in her living quarters.[11]

The marriage of Ida and Victor had never been a conventional one, and throughout the 1950s, many of the lovers whom Ida came to rely on for intimacy and support lived with her in her rooms.

In many ways, Ida's was an ideal personality to withstand the nihilism of post-war bohemia. She liked to socialise, meeting friends at the Colony (though the autocratic Muriel did not warm to the equally autocratic Ida), and watching Victor win in the 1947 chess championship at the Mandrake. But to her, alcohol was not the irresistible temptation which it was to many of the denizens of Soho. She might have liked to think of herself as a daring and eccentric figure but as her friend and former assistant John Kasmin recently remarked, she was a 'conventional bohemian', getting up in the morning when many of her friends were just going to bed, sleeping when Soho was just about to rouse.

John Christoforou's departure for France gave Victor Musgrave the opportunity to have his own art gallery in the building in Litchfield Street. He called it Gallery One, and opened in December 1953, with a Christoforou exhibition, prompting Quentin Bell to write in the *Listener* that the new enterprise was 'a small and adventurous establishment . . . just the place for the stoa of some new and outrageous philosophy of art, the kind of thing that will prove amazing, infuriating and yet compelling'.[12] 1954 was certainly a promising year in which to open a new gallery. The visual arts were expanding, a purchasing public was re-emerging, and interest from the critics was strong. The year saw the young Sandra Blow showing at Gimpel Fils in June, while Zwemmers mounted 'Painters Under Forty', a group show which included Patrick Heron. John Bratby held his first one-man show at the Beaux Arts Gallery, Roger Hilton was at Gimpels, and Ivon Hitchens was commissioned to paint murals at Cecil Sharpe House. Exhibitions at Gallery One included Kit Barker in September, and Martin Bradley in June.

The new venue soon became a respected, innovatory institution of the fifties. Many artists and critics liked it because the shows that Victor mounted did not depend on the work of an established coterie of British and European painters and sculptors. Some artists, like the painter Bridget Riley, began their careers as exhibitors with shows at Gallery One; others, who perhaps would not have been taken seriously in Cork Street, found that Victor Musgrave had an

Patrick Heron, painter and writer, 1954

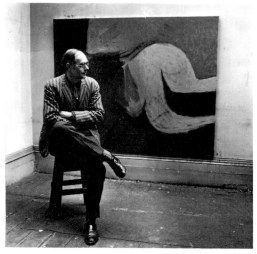

Roger Hilton, painter, late 1950s

open mind to experimentalism. Victor himself, charming but not obsequious, an intelligent man but not a manipulator, was much liked by those he worked with, and those who knew him during the fifties remember clearly that many people better off than himself were willing to assist him and to back the new enterprise. To some extent, Ida lived in the shadow of Gallery One for the remainder of the decade, though the presence of Victor in her life was to provide constant stimulus and vital information about the literary and visual arts communities which she wished to document.

One Litchfield Street resident who witnessed the beginning of Gallery One and the expansion of Ida's career in photography was the writer Bill Hopkins, himself to become a well-known figure of the decade. Hopkins took rooms with Ida and Victor in 1952:

My rent subsidised the gallery and their living. They were both as poor as church mice. The gallery had bare floor-boarding. It was a very, very amateurish space, and we shared meals on many a day, simply because there wasn't enough money to go around.[13]

Bill Hopkins was a close observer of Ida's struggles for recognition during the fifties, and the obstacles which lay in her path:

Ida Kar was in an ersatz profession called photography, which was not accepted as one of the arts. Indeed, we all regarded photography very much as a semi-swindle. Ida was always looked on as an interloper in the arts. It was thought pretentious of her to represent herself as an artist, and in that sense, I think she paid a very dear price for being a forerunner ... By mixing in the world of the arts, she put herself up against the very fortifications. If Ida was here today, she would say exactly what I am saying now, and with much bitterness. She was put down continually.... None of us accepted photography in those days as an art, and that was made very clear to Ida Kar. By everybody. If not directly, in their manner. If goaded, in conversation, directly, in speech. I've seen Ida cry over this. She couldn't get any subsidies or backing off anyone. Nobody knew she was a major artist. She had no money and no publicity. Nothing. It pushed her into a three-crisis-a-day routine.[14]

Life in Soho for Ida Kar, the flamboyant Armenian eccentric, could be comfortable and fulfilling; for Ida Kar, the serious photographer, craving recognition and respect, it consisted of endless frustration. The painter Francis Newton Souza, whom Ida

Francis Newton Souza, photographed by Ida in London, mid-1950s

Bill Hopkins, writer, London, early 1950s

met through Gallery One, also noticed how women photographers in London lacked status: 'Although there were noted women photographers like Margaret Bourke White in America, fotogs (sic) were negative in England. Lensmen, yes, lenswomen, no; female paparazzi, not at all.'[15]

Bill Hopkins remembers Ida with great warmth as: 'a wonderful woman, she will always remain in my memory. She wasn't a chameleon. She didn't try to charm anyone. She was always herself. Always Ida Kar. She filled the room with enormous warmth and laughter and mockery. She was a wonderful companion.'[16]

But alongside this personal affection, he recalls all too well how she could be viewed by the community in which she lived; in bohemia, as much as anywhere else during the fifties one's worth was adjudged by what one had to sell as much as by what one had to give away:

Ida had nothing to peddle. She couldn't peddle photography because that was scorned. She couldn't peddle sex because she wasn't in that business. All she could do was peddle abrasive ideas that no one wanted to hear anyway. A middle-aged, dumpy, foreign woman who was too self-opinionated by half. She was a bizarre, grotesque monster with highly unfashionable practices trying to push an ersatz commercial business called photography into a very sacred enclosure in which people lived and died for the arts. The most reactionary people were in the arts themselves. So when we were reactionary, she had no other harbour. It was very sad. All she could really have done was to go on to Trafalgar Square and photograph people feeding pigeons.[17]

F. N. Souza glimpsed too the tragic beneath Ida's ebullient façade: 'One might think of Ida Kar as one of those oddball characters from the "Lost Generation" in Paris in the 20s . . . I think of [her] as a mysterious ghostly character from Gogol's novels.'[18]

Misogyny also had its special place behind the looking glass which led to the *demi-monde*, as Bill Hopkins remembers:

Those times were very scathing. It was a caustic atmosphere. Even women painters were not that acceptable. Women had a nasty smell about them that they were trying to crawl into the art world under a false flag. They were put down and degraded. Their sanity was always questioned. If they were in agreement with dominant figures, then they were sane. If they were opposed to everyone, then they were insane.[19]

During the early fifties, however, Ida had great expectations of life and art. She had begun her long series of photographs of artists and writers in 1953, and she planned to hold an exhibition at Gallery One towards the end of 1954. To establish herself in the eyes of her peers as a portraitist active within seminal cultural circles, she used a photograph which she had taken of Jacob Epstein sculpting a head of Bertrand Russell for her 1953 Christmas card. At the beginning of 1954, she wrote to a number of British artists to ask for sittings, and she included Victor Pasmore, Lynn Chadwick, William Scott, Ivon Hitchens, Barbara Hepworth and Reg Butler on her list. She crossed the Channel to make portraits of Marc Chagall, Camille Bombois, Giacometti and Le Corbusier. Her studies of Henry Moore at his workshop in Much Hadham also date from this period.

In 1954, Ida met many people, and established some important connections. She began a correspondence with Ivon and Mollie Hitchens which lasted for the next decade, and she became friendly with Lynn Chadwick, spending a weekend with the sculptor and his family in the spring. Ida decided that her exhibition should consist of forty portraits of artists, twenty from France and twenty from Britain. By the summer of 1954, she had made all but ten of them.

Lack of financial backing for her project was then, as it was to be in the years to come, a pressing problem. She asked the paper and film manufacturers Agfa to give her printing paper for exhibition prints, and when none was forthcoming, explored possibilities of buying Kodak Bromesko or Ilford Plastika in Germany, in order to avoid British purchase tax. In June, Kodak offered to sponsor her show by providing paper, but all the remaining expenses had to be met from her own small income.

The struggle to make ends meet was a fairly constant one in the Musgrave–Kar household, but Ida was not daunted. She was encouraged by the response to her portraits. Most of her sitters liked them (although the writer Doris Lessing recalled later that she thought that Ida's portrait had made her look too glamorous). The painter Ivon Hitchens took a great interest in the photographs which Ida sent to him, writing to her in May 1954 with detailed comments about printing and cropping, and suggesting that she should include Patrick Heron in her series. Behind Ida's ebullient façade, there was, undeniably, tension and lack of certainty. The artist William Scott, who was photographed by her in 1954, remembers that Ida was shy and nervous when she posed him[20].

Her visits to artists at their homes sometimes involved long and complicated journeys by train and bus across the English

Ivon Hitchens, painter, Sussex, 1954

Display window for Ida's exhibition, 'Forty Artists from Paris and London', shown at Gallery One in 1954. (*Private collection*)

countryside. When she travelled to France, she did so as cheaply as possible, often buying tickets for cargo boats. In her forty-sixth year, strong and vigorous though she was, the pressure was considerable, and drew her energies away from routine studio and theatrical work, which had provided her with a basic income.

Despite all the obstacles, the exhibition prints were completed, and the show, entitled 'Forty Artists from Paris and London' opened at Gallery One in October 1954. The poster showed Ida's portrait of Marc Chagall, and Victor perfected an elegant signature for the selected photographs – spare and spiky, it was used by Ida throughout her career, and passed as her own[21]. After the opening night, she waited anxiously for the reviews to come in. What few there were were bound to disappoint: 'The practice of photographing artists is a popular one these days, and Miss Kar does it better than most ... though Kenneth Armitage looks almost too much like Britain's answer to Gregory Peck, the photographs usually manage to convey the essentials of character' was the main thrust of the report in *Arts News and Review* and apart from some biographical information in the *Manchester Guardian*, little else was said. Ida was caught in a singular trap. If she photographed celebrities or near-celebrities, then she knew that people would come to see her work, if only to judge her competence as a maker of likenesses. But while she gained a public, she also courted the possibility of being regarded as some kind of publicist, a celebrity photographer manqué. Her 'celebrities' were not, however, celebrated enough to be newsworthy, so her portraits were not able to assure her a good income from sales to the press. She was also lacking in business sense, or any real understanding of the workings of the media, and was not able to direct her photographs to the people and organisations able to buy them. Unlike other photographers who photographed the well known, she had no pre-war reputation on which to build, no network of contacts. Although already middle-aged, Ida was a fledgling photographer when compared with workers like Cecil Beaton and Angus McBean, who had built their careers in the innovatory inter-war decades. A persistent, determined, skilled and knowing photographer, Ida Kar was in some danger of becoming merely a Soho character.

Another continuing irony in Ida's life was the way in which her strength of personality, while enabling her to achieve many of her aims in photography, at the same time caused many of those who would have helped or employed her to turn away towards other more manageable image-makers. Ida saw photography as a conflict

Jack Smith, painter, London, 1959

Sandra Blow, painter, London, 1955

between portrayer and portrayed, and as she once wrote (in an unpublished typescript):

To produce an interesting work an artist needs a change, sometimes an overwhelming reception, real contact or dislike, arrogance or bad temper. It is only indifference which gives very little chance to be stimulated. When I photographed Brendan Behan, one moment I had the impression that he was going to slap my face, next to kick me.

Stimulating as this might have been for the creative process, it also established Ida as difficult and temperamental in the eyes of picture editors. It was a confrontational approach rare in the British tradition, in which photographers had customarily watched and waited rather than directed and imposed.

For many of her sitters though, her method was impressive. The painter Jack Smith, photographed by Ida in the late fifties, was convinced of her sureness of approach: 'Her method of working was precise and she knew exactly what quality she wished to convey.'[22] Another young artist, Sandra Blow, remembered Ida as 'intense, preoccupied with what she was doing, authoritative'.[23] Bridget Riley, who held her first one-woman exhibition at Gallery One in 1962, recalls that when Ida photographed her, the session was conducted 'with great intensity and concentration'.[24] William Gear, portrayed by Ida during the course of his 1954 exhibition at the South London Art Gallery, noticed that she took great pains to achieve precisely the poses which she wanted.[25] On rare occasions, Ida would allow a portrait session to be organised by the sitter. F. N. Souza, whose first Gallery One exhibition immediately followed Ida's own in 1954, was photographed by her many times from 1957 to 1962, and often arranged his own pose and setting for the photographs.[26]

The cramped, decaying rooms at Litchfield Street were increasingly unsuited to Ida and Victor's needs, and in 1955 they moved into a large corner building in D'Arblay Street in the heart of Soho, near to Berwick Street where Ida liked to buy her fruit and vegetables, and just around the corner from the pubs, clubs and cafés where the artists and writers of Soho gathered. Soho was an intricate tangle of streets, squares and byways, its shops and eating places exotic yet traditional. More than just a place where one might escape from the dourness of post-war London, it became a talisman against the forces of philistinism so closely observed by those, many of them young and inexperienced, who flocked to it in the post-war

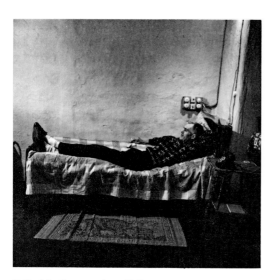

Colin MacInnes, writer, 1960

years. It became the obvious source material for much of fifties'
metropolitan fiction, often used to tell the tale of a journey from
innocence to experience. Its various well-known characters were
parodied and re-parodied, to the point where the real can become
indistinguishable from the fictional. Victor and Ida's new Soho
residence brought them to the very centre of the myth. Bill Hopkins,
their Litchfield Street tenant, had left the household to travel in
Europe, and the young writer Colin MacInnes (later to publish the
fifties classic *Absolute Beginners*, which incidentally, featured a
photographer as its central character) became their new lodger. In
D'Arblay Street, Gallery One was able to have a larger space, and
Ida acquired three rooms on the top floor, which she made into a
bedroom, sitting-room and studio. In the basement, she had a small
darkroom.

Improved as their situation was, Ida and Victor still had many
problems. They were still desperately short of money, and neither
of their enterprises was producing a substantial enough income to
alleviate their problems. Gallery One had some backers, but Ida
had none, and although her work was being published, she had few
commissions and no plans for future exhibitions.

As pressing as any other problem was the increasingly stressed
relationship between Ida and Victor. Dissimilar in habits and
attitude, they both adopted other friendships, pursued other
interests, while still relying on each other for help and comfort. Ida,
who loved as she found, embarked on a series of relationships with
a variety of men, regardless of any disparity in age, class or
occupation. Many of these emotional and sexual adventures caused
her some pain, but they became an indispensable part of her life as
she grew into middle age.

Unexpectedly, a new catalyst, in the shape of the twenty-one-
year-old John Kasmin (now a prominent international art dealer
and gallery owner) made itself felt in the household. In 1956,
Kasmin returned from a lengthy stay in New Zealand:

> I came back in the spring of 1956, and within the first couple of
> months of being back, I'd found that I liked the company of
> writers and painters, the people hanging around at the York
> Minster and David Archer's bookshop and the Colony Room
> and the Caves de France. One of the first art world groupings I
> got into was Victor Musgrave's Gallery One ... Quite an
> interesting group of people would meet there, particularly in the
> afternoons, when Ida would have a tea party going ... I thought
> this looked like the perfect lodge for me to nest in. I had very

little money, and Victor couldn't afford an assistant, but somehow, despite that, I did in fact enter the household, within a few weeks of meeting them.[27]

John Kasmin became Ida's most valuable associate. For a brief period he worked as her assistant but quickly took over her business affairs and the promotion of her career, at the same time working as Victor's assistant in the running of Gallery One. He was one of the few people in Ida's life who had both an open mind about and a keen interest in the medium of photography, and saw her as 'a fabulous portraitist of the old school, with instinctive magic'. He realised that she was neither taking advantage of existing opportunities, nor recognising new ones. Although the household was 'in emotional turmoil, a passionate sort of place'. Kasmin quickly constructed for Ida a photography business within which her skills could be utilised to provide her with greater exposure and an improved income. For Ida, who had fought a long and hopeless battle to be considered an artist, it must have come as a relief to be a photographer again.

Kasmin, looking for the ways in which Ida could diversify without any sacrifice of quality, attempted, with some success, to divert Ida into photo-reportage. With television still in its infancy, the public relied heavily on published photographs for insight, education and entertainment. The photojournalistic tradition was still alive in Britain (although the legendary magazine *Picture Post* was to close in 1957), Ida Kar was a skilled and acute practitioner, so the inevitable next move seemed to be to bring Ida and the media together. She abandoned her cumbersome plate camera and bought a smaller format Rolleiflex, and, prompted by Kasmin, began to make picture stories about London life, many of which were used by the *Tatler*. A substantial amount of work was also placed with the *Observer* newspaper. She photographed the shopkeepers and customers of the Royal Opera Arcade, documented 'exotic' religions in London, and produced lively and atmospheric pictures of performers and audience at the Metropolitan Music Hall. At their best, these pieces of photojournalism bring to the fore Ida's unerring ability to imbue her photography with a hardness and a sharpness which eschews utterly any idea of whimsy or sentimentality. Her Royal Opera Arcade shopkeepers emerge from her photographs as bizarre, looming creatures guarding their treasure caves of jewels and fine china, her loiterers at the Edgeware Music Hall are solemn citizens of the *demi-monde*, emerging from shadows to pools of light, disturbing and mysterious.

A shopkeeper in the Royal Opera Arcade, London, mid-1950s

Ida and a friend exploring the Harz mountains, nd.
(*Private collection*)

Ida's ability to see patterning in whatever she photographed, to construct her own scenarios within a sitter's own environment, stood her in good stead when she took up photojournalism. Kasmin quickly became the arranger of Ida's professional life. From 1956 to 1958, he would

find out who was in town, playwrights, and film-stars and actresses who might interest us. One of my jobs was to invent business. I would telephone and say I'd been commissioned by a newspaper to interview them and photograph them. I'd just bluff it. Whether it was Tennessee Williams or T. S. Eliot, I would just telephone, and with most of the calls I would arrange visits. We collected authors and artists. We'd always give a couple of shots to Camera Press who would sell them in a routine way for a single column to newspapers all over the world. We'd sell a portrait and make a story out of someone being in town. We also sold prints to the people we photographed. That was another source of revenue.[28]

Kasmin discovered that attending a portrait session with Ida could be a testing experience. Adept in her own work, she sometimes had little or no idea of the achievements of some of those whom she photographed. To her, they were all just sitters, distinguished perhaps because she had chosen to photograph them, but treated in no accordance with their fame or excellence.

Ida was exactly the same whoever she was with. She was distinctly unintellectual. She *was* able to respect sculptors and photographers more than writers. For me, there were moments of the most excruciating embarrassment. The way she treated T. S. Eliot – she obviously had no idea what he wrote. There were moments when I couldn't believe it. I would think, 'How could I possibly be doing this with Ida for a living?' Then we would have a terrible shouting match out on the street – she had this tremendous, strong, hooting voice.[29]

Utterly absorbed in whatever she was doing, Ida was intent on creating her own fame rather than assessing that of others. When photographing, she became totally absorbed and frequently autocratic. She created at times situations which were uneasy for her sitters and for those who assisted her in her photography. For many who did business with her, she exuded all the qualities of that familiar stereotype – the difficult woman. Improved as her career was, however, she was able to begin to consider new and exciting plans.

By the late fifties, Ida had begun a series of extended working visits to the Soviet Union and Eastern Europe. In 1957, she made her first trip to Armenia, a homeland which she had not seen since infancy. She had obtained a commission from the *Observer*, but undoubtedly, the impetus behind her visit was as much personal as it was professional. Her parents had returned to Erevan (the major city of Armenia), they were ageing, and she was anxious to re-establish a relationship which had undergone a break of almost a decade. She spent the first week of her trip in Paris, travelling by rail and sea from London, staying with her old friend Marie-Thérèse Lelio. She was excited about the opportunities which her Armenian visit presented, writing to Victor at the beginning of August that she would make him 'rich and famous one day', and imploring him to 'please have patience'.[30] Her jubilation evaporated rapidly when she found herself on a slow and uncomfortable long-distance train, making its way towards the USSR. With her own peculiar blend of exaggeration and insensitivity, she compared her rudimentary travelling conditions to those suffered by 'deported Jewish people'.[31] Widely travelled as she was, she was still amazed by her fellow Armenians, making the trip to see friends and relatives:

> The things I have already seen are like things I have only read about or seen in the cinema. They are heroic. Most of them are very old people. Most are illiterate. I think that only Armenians who have suffered are capable of such things.[32]

Travelling in the USSR, late 1950s

Ida saw her trip to Armenia as a breakthrough. Sitting in her cramped compartment, she wrote to Victor, 'I must make money and a big success, after all the money I have spent, and all this trouble.'[33]

At Erevan railway station, a huge crowd of people had gathered to meet the visitors. There was complete chaos, and even the contingent of police were unable to restore order. Ida's mother, who was old and ill, fainted in the crush, but Ida was delighted to see her father little changed. The first few days in Armenia more than made up for the strain of the journey, and the money worries which had occupied her so much in London receded. It was indeed ironic that here, in her homeland, she was what she had never been in any of her adopted countries, an honoured guest.

By the middle of August, Ida Kar was comfortably installed in the Hotel Armenia in the centre of Erevan. She was provided with a government car and driver and given much assistance in

Ida at work with the Rolleiflex, USSR, 1957

Armenia, 1957

organising her itinerary. Her knowledge of both Armenian and Russian enabled her to speak with her fellow countrymen and women without having to resort to the use of a translator. The sun shone and people in the street smiled and stopped to talk. The pressures of London life must have seemed many miles away. Excited and optimistic, she wrote to Victor, assuring him that she was at last about to be able to banish all their financial worries. The Armenians had invited her to mount an exhibition of her work at the end of August, and more than anything else, Ida loved to have her photographs displayed in public. She was also determined that her photographs should have an educative value when she brought them home:

> People who have come from outside come deaf and blind to visit the Soviet Union. I am preparing a glorious exhibition. Really, from Cartier Bresson's photographs, you can have no idea what it is really like. I feel now that I would like to get up on a chair in Hyde Park and speak to the people of England about the Soviet people. We must unite our forces to ensure peace.[34]

Ida did not limit her work in Armenia to portraiture. In the last week of August she visited a peasant community outside Erevan, where she sat around an open fire and ate traditional Armenian food. She used six rolls of film to photograph the village gathering, and gave away all her bracelets to the shy peasant women who hid in their huts as the festivities went on. The heat was intense and the country roads so dusty that the travellers seemed to be 'almost eating the dust'. But Ida was ecstatic and euphoric, and decided that after the trip was over she would 'travel all over the world among simple people and photograph their lives'.[35]

Simplicity was not, however, the only virtue which Ida valued in Armenia. She found a thriving artistic community in Erevan, and much welcome respect for the art of photography. According to her own accounts, many of Armenia's most celebrated writers and artists were eagerly awaiting a meeting with her, and on encountering her, she recalled, 'they simply looked at me with wonder'.[36]

Ida Kar enjoyed fame and celebration only a very few times in her career, and in these few summer weeks in Erevan, she was treated like a great lady, an artist with a camera, an Armenian who had met and worked with some of the great names in the history of Western art. A fantasy which she had nurtured for years became briefly a reality. When letters arrived for her from London

Ida sat for many sculptors and painters during her visits to Armenia. This bust was made by Nikogos Nikogossian in Erevan, 1957

Armenia, 1957

reminding her of the emotional and financial battlefield which she had left behind in D'Arblay Street, she sympathised, but distantly. In Armenia, Ida was no longer on the outside, looking in. At last, she belonged.

The exhibition opened in Erevan on 29 August 1957. It was a great success, and Ida did not fall prey to modesty when she described it:

It is crowded every day, and when I am there, I am absolutely surrounded and asked all sorts of questions, technical and artistic. Every so often it comes to such a point that I have to go and rest. Yesterday I went to the theatre, but I was so tired that I could not enjoy it. Afterwards we had to walk a long way before we could find a taxi, and about a hundred people began to follow me and my parents. At last a taxi came to our rescue. It's a pity that I did not get a photograph of this, but I may try to get one, as it happens so often. I have become an heroic figure for them. They will never forget me. I dance the Armenian waltz beautifully, speak four languages and have spoken about my exhibition on the radio in Armenian. One day I am posing for a painter, the next for a sculptor ... I am becoming almost legendary. I am sculpted, painted and caricatured. I am loved by artists and especially by writers.[37]

So involved with her new life had Ida become, that even disturbing news from London concerning the infidelities of her current lover did not have much effect on her equilibrium: 'I have such an interesting life here, and such a wonderful and cultural people. I am working so hard here that I will not have time for anything unimportant [when I return]. Life is too short and too important.'[38]

Life for Ida in Armenia was indeed hectic. She woke at four in the morning to begin work and to avoid some of the intense heat, and was busy until the late evening. The Armenians had done much to make her feel welcome and comfortable, providing her with 'a lovely room, a little bathroom to myself, a desk and a telephone and plenty of fruit always on the table'.[39] She considered herself 'spoilt and loved by so many interesting but also simple people'.[40] She was intensely proud of her native country, and complained bitterly to Victor about the way in which European photographers (notably, she thought, Cartier Bresson) had portrayed the USSR as being 'a land of misery and dust'[41] and determined that her own photographs would help to redress the balance.

Bryan Robertson, gallery director, London, 1958

Cecil Beaton, photographer and designer, Wiltshire, 1960

Much as she would have liked to extend her visit, by the middle of September, she was making plans to return home. She sent Victor a cheque and asked him to organise a homecoming party. She intended to come back in style, travelling by air in national costume and bearing gifts of caviar and cognac for friends at home. From Erevan, Ida travelled to Moscow, and by the end of September, she was as thrilled about returning home as she had been about revisiting Armenia. Three hundred guests had been invited to her party, including many members of the Armenian community in London. A lonely week in Moscow was followed by an overnight stop in Paris, and on 9 October she boarded an Air France jet bound for London, and, she hoped, a new era.

The next three years were to be ones of intense activity. A meeting with Bryan Robertson (according to contemporary sources, this took place at the very homecoming party that Victor had organised on Ida's return from Armenia), the young, dynamic director of the Whitechapel Art Gallery had resulted in her being invited to prepare an exhibition. The prospect of such a show spurred her on to intensified photographic activity. In the spring of 1958, she was travelling again, this time with an assistant, to Moscow and Sweden. Back in London, she resumed her portraiture, photographing Sidney Nolan and making a cool, sharp picture of Bryan Robertson. In November, she visited Ivon Hitchens again, this time portraying him in colour amongst the luxuriant greenery of his Sussex garden.

The following year saw the beginning of a somewhat uneasy relationship between Ida and the fashion and portrait photographer Cecil Beaton. It is intriguing to imagine the first meeting between the two photographers, the elegant, worldly Beaton, photographer for *Vogue* magazine, portraitist of the Royal family, a celebrity in his own right, and the rumpled, outspoken Ida Kar, still struggling to achieve recognition. She photographed him in the conservatory of his country house in Wiltshire, picturing him as an isolated and severe figure amid the ornate structure of the glasshouse and its extravagant foliage. It survives as one of Ida's most moving portraits, and one which, without any overt manipulation, penetrates the dandy façade and speaks of ageing, sadness and loneliness. Beaton was not entirely pleased with the portrait, and he wrote to Ida:

I was a bit surprised at first to see myself standing in such a stiff, strange way. It is unlike any other photograph of me. I suppose it is an interesting slant and development. It was stupid of me not to put the hat on with more of a dash. There is a sitting one *I*

East Germany, 1959

like, but if you prefer the other, please do what you think fit. I would appreciate a little retouching.[42]

Though Beaton knew well the potency of the photographic process, he could still be alarmed by its ability to penetrate and to unveil.

By the summer of 1959, Ida was back in Armenia, but the magic and excitement of her first visit was never recaptured. She complained to Victor that the Armenians were badly organised, and to her friend Josef Herman that 'everyone was so *old*'.[43] In September, she travelled to East Germany, by way of Moscow, and once again found herself being treated as a much honoured visitor. The East Germans provided her with a car, a driver and an interpreter, as well as the use of a darkroom. She worked as hard as ever, spending whole days making contact prints of the film she had processed. Despite all her efforts, the photographs which she brought back from East Germany are amongst her least distinguished. Her position as a guest and the generosity of her hosts perhaps compromised her intentions as a reporter, and very early in her trip she was telephoning Kasmin in London to instruct him that her photographs should not 'be used in any way detrimental to East Germany'.[44] As ingenuous and as grateful as ever, Ida followed the advice of her hosts, and photographed what they advised her to photograph. She visited factories and shops and museums, but produced very little which rose above mere record. It was hardly a promising beginning to the great career in photojournalism which she had begun to envisage. In August 1959, her Armenian photographs were put on show in a one-woman exhibition at the Zentralen Haus der Deutsch-Sowjetischen Freundschaft in East Berlin, to an enthusiastic reception. But even Ida, with her immense belief in her own abilities, made very little use of her East German photographs in the years to come.

Although, in the late fifties, Ida contemplated another extended photographic visit abroad, this time to China, again as a guest of the government, the opening of her Whitechapel exhibition had been set for the spring of 1960 and she had much work to do. She began to complete her series of British artists and writers, abandoning for a time her documentary stance, and resorting again to her characteristic portraiture methods. Perhaps foreign travel had increased her confidence, perhaps the imposed breaks from portraiture had refined her ways of seeing, for the pictures which she produced in 1959 are some of her most significant. In these portraits, she seems to penetrate even more deeply into the fantastic

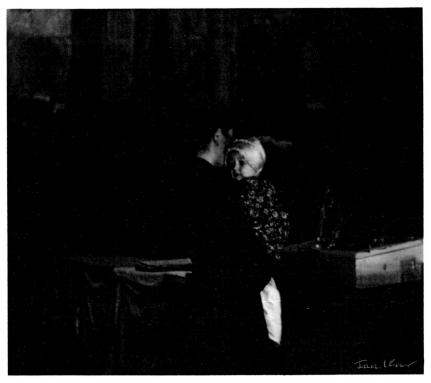

and idiosyncratic worlds of artists and writers. She photographed the painter John Bratby (page 153) against the jarring and colliding kaleidoscope of patterns which surrounded him in his studio. She visited Augustus John and portrayed an aged craftsman, proud and moving in painter's overalls. She confronted the writer Brendan Behan (page 119), and without posing or friendly chatter produced one of her most incisive images of the decade.

By 1960, Ida had produced the best work of her career. She was technically more accomplished, she saw opportunities more quickly, and was prepared to take greater risks with compositions and stylisation. But around her, everything was changing. Friends from Soho were dispersing – Bill Hopkins was in Europe, Kasmin was looking to the time when he would open his own art gallery, and other, younger photographers were poised to re-establish the medium as a vital cultural force. Although Ida Kar was to play her own important part in the revival of British photography the new decade was to bring her few real rewards.

Nevertheless, as she pondered over the selection of photographs for the Whitechapel show, set the prices for her prints, agonised over how she would meet all the bills for this eventually very costly project, her future seemed immensely promising.

CHAPTER THREE

In this purblind land

Photography in the 1950s and the Whitechapel exhibition

In 1951, an exasperated Angus McBean shared his thoughts on the current state of photography with the readers of the *Photography Year Book*:

> Photography still lags behind. Would-be exhibition photographers still have irresistible impulses to dress little girls in Kate Greenaway costumes, place them beside a spinet and call the picture 'Songs My Grandma Sang'. How I hate the boredom of the average exhibition room, with row upon row of pictures, sterile as the Chantry Bequest and as technically perfect. They will call them 'Carmen', 'The Captive', or perhaps 'The Dying Musician'.

As an imaginative, persuasive and stylistic tool, the medium had almost completely ceased to function in Britain. London, which had once been the centre of photographic innovation, had lost its energy and its importance. British photography was at a crossroads, and indecision and isolation were symptomatic of its state. Cecil Beaton, one of the foremost London experimentalists of the inter-war decades, wrote gloomily in his post-war diary:

> The war had given me an incentive to step out towards new photographic horizons, and to point my camera at more rugged aspects of life; but that incentive was now removed. Yet I did not want to go back to my old vomit. Enough of taking fashions on young models who survived just as long as their faces showed no sign of character, or of elderly, but rich harpies appearing as if butter would not melt in their terrible mouths. In what direction should I go now? What was my aim? What did I really want to do?[1]

For many, the decision had already been made during the war years. Radical British workers like John Havinden and Barbara Ker-Seymer abandoned photography completely on the outbreak

Lecturing, location unknown, early 1960s

of war. Their markets were gone, their materials rationed. Those who carried on, like the experimentalists Madame Yevonde and Helen Muspratt, were obliged to rely increasingly on routine studio portraiture to ensure their continued livelihoods. Those who had seen the new radical politics of the 1930s as an inspirational spur for some of their most significant work, found themselves, after 1939, in a political landscape changed out of all recognition. Workers like the documentarist Edith Tudor Hart, who had combined with the New Left to reveal the iniquities of slumland to a receptive public, were to find no niche among the official propagandists who emerged when war was declared.

For women photographers, the situation was particularly difficult. Many of those who had children left London when hostilities began. Photography was a reserved occupation, so women were not able to fill the gaps which might otherwise have been left by their male counterparts. Women photographers who joined the services were not diverted into photographic corps. For many skilled women within the medium, the beginning of the Second World War indicated the end of freedom of choice. Almost overnight, Britain re-assumed traditionalism.

Before the war, many hundreds of women had operated successfully as photographers in London and throughout Britain. When the war ended, few of these women appear to have continued in business. Those photographers, both male and female, whose practice had survived change and disruption, saw little to stimulate them as the forties and fifties progressed. While photography continued to play an important part in newspapers and magazines, as a recognised and accredited art form, its identity was lost. Just at the time that British painting and sculpture was enjoying an enormous revival, photography (uncatered for by the remit of the fledgling Arts Council of Great Britain) had become again that singular hybrid of craft and trade, with occasional pretensions to the artistic. No one whose opinion was held to be of any account acknowledged either photography's scope or its history. It was as if it had never been. The medium lacked status and it lacked stars. Although an infrastructure of a kind was still in place, with the Royal Photographic Society continuing to hold its annual exhibitions, and the camera clubs still active, the general picture was moribund. Major museums and galleries operated by the state or by local government were virtually united in their refusal to consider photography as worthy of either collection or exhibition, and photographic works, whether antiquarian or contemporary, had no value in the arts market place.

Ailing as the state of photography was, several key figures and institutions began to work, in their different ways, to prevent the total decline of the medium within British cultural circles. The collector, photographer and historian Helmut Gernsheim, whose huge collection contained works by many seminal British photographers, was the first, and by far the most important, of the post-war British-based writers on photography. In 1948, his survey of the work of the nineteenth-century portraitist Julia Margaret Cameron was published. In that same year, the Focal Press issued *The Man Behind the Camera*, reminding the public of the achievements of such workers as Angus McBean, Cecil Beaton and Wolfgang Suschitzky. The following year saw the publication of Gernsheim's *Lewis Carroll: Photographer*, a scholarly, well-researched exploration of the Victorian author's photographic archive. Forty years on, with the study of the history of photography accepted as a legitimate discipline, it is perhaps difficult to appreciate the importance of these publishing initiatives. Not how-to-do-it instruction manuals, nor how-I-did-it autobiographies, such projects formed the first serious post-war attempt to define and explore the history of British photography, and their importance cannot be overestimated.

Few other books appeared during the 1950s to attract the attention of photographers who looked for more than technical guidance. In 1951, a series of images by Paul Nash was issued by Faber as *The Fertile Image*, and in 1956, the Harvill Press announced the publication of *Gala Day London*, an important initiative showing the work of the documentarist Iziz Bidermanns. The 1957 Penguin Books catalogue saw the inclusion of Eric de Mare's *Photography*, and later that year, the Fountain Press began to distribute Arthur Rothstein's *Photojournalism*. It was not until almost the end of the decade that Oxford University Press produced Helmut and Alison Gernsheim's *The History of Photography*, which explored the history of the medium up to 1914. Photographic publishing was at its best sporadic, while many years of the post-war decades saw not a single new initiative. Workers like Cecil Beaton, whose careers in publishing were already well-established before the war, still managed to get their work into print; seven publications devoted to Beaton's photography appeared during the fifties, including his *Photobiography* (1951), *Persona Grata* (1953) and the 1950s classic *The Face of the World*, issued by Weidenfeld and Nicolson in 1957.

Opportunities to see either historical or contemporary photography on exhibition were also rare in the fifties. The beginning of the decade saw an encouraging initiative in the shape of 'Masterpieces of Victorian Photography', a major exhibition at the Victoria and Albert Museum drawn from Gernsheim's collection which opened to the public in May 1951. The staging of the show did not indicate any real enthusiasm for photography by the Museum's hierarchy, and it was not until 1968 that the Victoria and Albert promoted another large photography project, and even this – a Cartier Bresson exhibition so successful that, during its showing, entrance to the exhibition gallery had to be strictly controlled to avoid overcrowding – was made possible only by the artist's generosity and extreme penny-pinching by its advocates inside the Museum.

Admirers of photojournalism did have a few opportunities to see the work of acknowledged leaders of the field displayed as exhibitions. In 1952, the Institute of Contemporary Arts in Dover Street advertised a showing of Cartier Bresson photographs, and strenuous efforts by the then editor of *Photography* magazine, Norman Hall, ensured that a larger exhibition of the French photographer's work was seen at the RBA gallery in January 1957. Another important chance to see world-renowned photography came in 1955, when the Royal Festival Hall played host to the massive 'Family of Man' exhibition, on tour around the world after its initial showing in New York. The show had already attracted large American audiences to its opening at New York's Museum of Modern Art, and its impact on the London public was significant. The *Picture Post* photographer, Godfrey Thurston Hopkins, went to see the exhibition during its time on the South Bank, and remembered that:

> It was incredible. There were giant enlargements, free-standing – they didn't put them on the walls. They were on tubular poles, great big enlargements that you walked around. It wasn't just the kind of photographs they were displaying which was so remarkable, it was the way they displayed them.[2]

Thurston Hopkins also recalled the potency of such large-scale exhibitions, and their effect not only on photographers, but on the media industry: 'All the advertising people in London, all the art directors, went to the "Family of Man". Almost to a man, almost overnight, they said, "this is the kind of photography we need to sell our goods". It brought in a new era of advertising photography.'[3]

The boldness and assertiveness of the 'Family of Man' brought a corresponding upsurge of confidence on the part of British photographers. Although some still mourned the passing of the expansive decades between the wars, others saw signs of a revival. In the 1955 edition of the *Photography Year Book* (which, under the editorship of Norman Hall and Basil Burton, strove to improve standards for the medium), the editors noted that:

> Everywhere, photographers seem to be growing in their appreciation of design ... With this evergrowing urge to make photographs there comes too, a widening appreciation of pictures. There is evidence among the post-war youth of different countries that this tremendous surge of interest in photography will bring many new artists to the surface.

Hall and Burton did much to introduce their readers to the work being produced by American and European photographers; in the mid-1950s, they published, in the *Photography Year Book*, works by, among others, Cartier Bresson, Edward Weston, Willy Ronis, Berenice Abbott and Ansel Adams.

The hostility of the major museums and galleries to photography still worked against the possibility of a major revival of the medium. While in the United States, one-person shows and retrospectives were devoted to the work of Barbara Morgan (at the International Museum of Photography, Rochester, New York in 1955) to Andreas Feininger (at the Smithsonian Institute, Washington, in 1957) and to Paul Strand (at the Museum of Modern Art, New York, in 1956), the British bastions of the Tate, the Victoria and Albert and the National Portrait Gallery (to say nothing of regional museums and art galleries) still stood strong against the possibility of an invasion by photography.

British photographers who wished to show their work to the public had to look to alternative, or increasingly, to corporate venues. In 1957, Adolf Morath's work was shown at the Tea Centre in Lower Regent Street, John Deakin mounted his Paris exhibition in 1956 at David Archer's bookshop in Greek Street, Soho and the young Roger Mayne showed in 1956 in the Members' Room of the Institute of Contemporary Arts.

Depressing as the situation was for would-be exhibitors, some cause for optimism was to be found in the activities of the Kodak organisation. Since the beginning of the fifties, Kodak had been organising exhibitions to be shown at its London headquarters. The Kodak Gallery, under the leadership of Robert Lassam (now curator of the Fox Talbot Museum), became a vital showplace for British photography. In 1957, Kodak House mounted Eric Hosking's 'Looking at Birds', which it subsequently toured, and, as

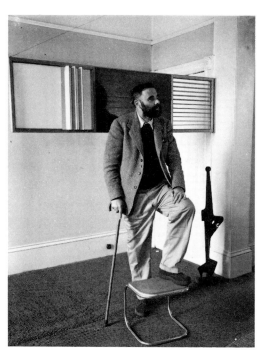

Victor Pasmore, artist, 1954

the fifties and sixties progressed, singled out for public attention some of the photographers – including Anthony Armstrong-Jones, Terence Donovan and Clive Arrowsmith – who were to lead the photographic renaissance of the post-war years.

By the time that Ida Kar's exhibition opened at the Whitechapel Gallery in March 1960, a fragile but real framework for the photographic revival was in place. For Ida, whose last show had been in 1954, at Gallery One, the time seemed right to arrange something quite stupendous.

'Believe me,' wrote Ida to Bryan Robertson some two weeks before her Whitechapel exhibition opened to the public, 'we are going to make this show the most exciting photographic event since the "Family of Man".'[4]

Ida knew the Whitechapel well; she had photographed L. S. Lowry there in the mid-1950s, and was a frequent visitor to its exhibitions. Throughout the second half of the 1950s, the Whitechapel had mounted a series of highly innovative shows, many of them featuring the work of Ida's friends and sitters (Josef Herman in 1956, Jack Smith in 1959, and others). It was instrumental in bringing new and experimental visual arts to the public's attention. The Gallery's 1956 series of exhibitions, 'This Is Tomorrow', brought into prominence the work of artists such as Richard Hamilton, Eduardo Paolozzi and Victor Pasmore, while in 1958, the programme included a one-man show by the controversial American painter, Jackson Pollock. To exhibit at the Whitechapel was, for Ida, an acknowledgement that she was indeed an artist in the company of her peers. She determined that her exhibition should, in scope and in size, equal any of the painting shows that had hung on the Whitechapel's walls during the past decade.

The gallery's size, status and situation all appealed to Ida. Set up by philanthropic bequest to bring the best of the visual arts to the East End of London, it was free of the strictures of civil servants, yet at the same time relatively unconstricted by commercial pressures. Situated on the Whitechapel High Street, with the public library on one side, Blooms kosher restaurant on the other, and just a few steps away from the underground station, the gallery co-existed with the bustle of one of the East End's busiest street markets. For Ida, who loved activity and oddity, and who would hold a conversation with anyone who would listen, it must have seemed a fine place for an art gallery. Inside, it was spacious and peaceful, with high ceilings and wooden floors. Ida's planned exhibition would be the first photography show to be held at the

Whitechapel since the war, and for the next two years, she exerted all her imagination and her energy towards ensuring that it would be a phenomenon rare indeed in the medium's contemporary history.

The date of the exhibition was not confirmed until the summer of 1958, when Bryan Robertson wrote to Ida to say that he would be 'delighted to organise a large exhibition of your photographic work in 1960 . . . I think the exhibition should consist of portraits of one kind and another, possibly mostly artists – and that these should be offset by a series of photographs of landscapes or of people disporting themselves in landscapes or with city backgrounds'.[5] Ida, fresh from her Armenian experience, had wanted one section of the show to be devoted to photographs from the Soviet Union, but Robertson had disagreed: 'I think that the photographs of landscapes and people in landscapes should be of a general kind, covering several countries and backgrounds. . . . However this is worked, I am sure that it should not consist entirely of Armenia.'[6]

The new relationship with Bryan Robertson and the Whitechapel opened up a number of possibilities, which Ida, desperate for new commissions and professional advancement, was as anxious as ever to make use of. She suggested to Robertson that she should undertake all the photographs for a book which he was planning about British sculptors, and was dismayed when Robertson counselled caution:

> I am sure that it would be best to wait for me to talk to each one of the sculptors concerned and find out from them how they feel about being photographed by yourself. I have already encountered one sculptor who wants very much to be represented by a photograph taken by somebody else. You can certainly take it that I shall use as many as possible of the marvellous photographs you've already taken of British sculptors; but I feel that I should talk to everyone concerned before we go any further with the idea of you doing the complete book.[7]

However, the Whitechapel connection was a valuable one for Ida and she made as much use of it as she could. In 1958, Bryan Robertson issued her with a letter of recommendation to be used during the course of future foreign travel:

> Miss Kar is one of the most distinguished and gifted photographers in England, with a first-class reputation. Her exhibition will be elaborately presented and will undoubtedly be greeted in all

quarters as an important event in the artistic and cultural life of London ... in the course of her travels, Miss Kar may be given all facilities in the course of her work, which will be of direct interest to her forthcoming exhibition. These travels will include Soviet Russia, and both Miss Kar and myself hope that in Russia it will be possible for her to photograph not only places and objects of historical or cultural or social interest, but also officials and artists of all kinds, at various levels.[8]

Clearly, the period before the show was an anxious, as well as an exhilarating one for Ida. She confided her worries to her friends, and in December 1959, Ivon Hitchens was writing to reassure her that 'clearly the show is ON', but cautioning her to 'waste no time, but to push on at once. You will probably find the time *shorter* than I know you want or need'.[9]

The exhibition, as Ida had planned it, was an expensive project, and much of the money had to be found from her own resources. Although, through Robert Lassam, she had secured a gift of paper from Kodak for her exhibition prints, she had still to pay the Autotype company to print the massive enlargements, and the catalogue which she planned to publish was to cost more than £1,000. 'It cost her her shirt,' remembered her friend Josef Herman. 'She insisted on scale, and this was expensive. She insisted on good craftsmanship, and this was very expensive. So she worked her head off to pay for it.'[10] Ida hoped that she would be able to sell works from the exhibition and recover some of her costs. With this in mind, she determined on a strategy of offering only limited numbers of each photograph for sale, hoping that she would create an air of exclusivity around her work, and at the same time, dispel the popular idea that photographs had no real value, because they are infinitely reproducible.

At long last, in the spring of 1960, the long process of selection, printing, retouching, mounting and hanging was finally over. Ida Kar's exhibition opened to the public on Tuesday, 22 March 1960. The catalogue listed one hundred and fourteen works, mainly portraits of British and European artists and writers, with a scattering of Russian and Armenian studies. Ida was a good judge of her own work, and in the show were many of her most incisive portraits of the new cultural movers of the fifties as well as portraits of venerated workers from both Britain and Europe. She chose portraits of Reg Butler (page 143), Craigie Aitchison (page 116), Elisabeth Frink, Shelagh Delaney (page 154), and Sandra Blow (page 124) to represent the young and the new. Her friend and

Elisabeth Frink, sculptor, 1956

Sir John Rothenstein in the sculpture hall at the Tate Gallery, London, 1960

At the Whitechapel Exhibition, 1960. Ida is standing in front of her portrait of Shostakovitch

supporter Colin MacInnes (page 103), photographed by Ida lounging in quintessential bedsitterland, was given a prominent position. Of all Ida's portraits from the fifties, it exemplifies finely and accurately the surface and atmosphere of the English bohemia. On show too was her portrait of two Soho friends, Brian and Susan Robbins. The couple posed in their basement coffee bar, and are seen in the photograph as chic, modern and invulnerably young, foregrounded by a line of Cona coffee jugs and thrown into relief by the rough-hewn walls and angular *objets d'art*.

From her portraits of writers she selected Laurie Lee, loose and half-bashful before his collection of pin-ups, and Brendan Behan, tie askew, angrily confronting the camera. Some old friends from Gallery One appeared on the Whitechapel's walls – John Christoforou (page 84), photographed in 1954 and enlarged to an enormous four feet by five feet, and F. N. Souza, an even larger print from a late fifties negative. The photograph which marked the beginning of Ida's work as a portraitist of the arts community in Britain occupied pride of place as the first plate in the catalogue, showing a workmanlike Jacob Epstein sculpting a head of the jaunty and debonair Bertrand Russell in 1953.

From the worlds of galleries and museums, Ida included her cool, precise and highly structured photograph of Bryan Robertson (page 125); very young, very male and very elegant in bow tie and striped shirt against a white background with intersecting lines. Her portrait of John Rothenstein, director of the Tate Gallery, showed him, gargoyle-like miniaturised by the bleak columns of the Tate's sculpture hall, surrounded by what seemed like miles of marble. She had included a number of photographs made in Armenia, including a dramatic study of a radar screen, a 34″ × 26″ blow-up of her portrait of Avetik Isahakian (1957) and a close-up photograph of her father, Melkon Karamian, made during that first visit in 1957.

The Whitechapel exhibition was more, for Ida, than a mere passing show. It represented the pinnacle of her achievement, the fulfilment of her most dear ambitions. The portraits, hung on the white walls of the gallery, were both her past and her future. As she advanced into middle age, they were the justification for all of the effort, all the investment, all the pain of the preceding fifteen years. For Ida, the exhibition had the potency of a magic spell, which, when worked, would take her from penury to riches, from obscurity to fame.

Ida believed that the exhibition would bring her fame; but even more than that, she hoped and expected that it would bring her employment. Not the essentially erratic and opportunistic freelancing which she had pursued throughout the fifties, but a secure and salaried post on the staff of some prestigious newspaper or magazine. She imagined that she too would become a prima donna of photography like the great Margaret Bourke White (who was the only photographer at *Life* magazine to have her own office with her nameplate on the door). Sadly, the contrast between the American photojournalist and the British portraitist could not have been greater. Their only real similarity was their unswerving belief in their own excellence. Bourke White had learnt to play to the public gallery, Ida still directed her photographs towards a critical and cynical elite. Bourke White had learnt to manipulate and exploit as well as, or better than, any man; poor Ida Kar, for all her egoism, had still to assimilate the most basic lessons of the politics of power.

Friends like Josef Herman realised the danger of Ida's great expectations:

> After the exhibition, she lived in a world of illusionary expectations. She expected quite a lot of Prince Charmings to arrive and solve all her problems. No Prince Charming arrived. No editor came to knock at her door. Really, quite literally, nothing happened. It was nice, there was good press coverage, there was great admiration for her, but this was about all.[11]

The *Evening Standard* sent John Moynihan, one of its diarists, on a celebrity spotting mission to Ida's private view at the Whitechapel. Pressing his way through the assembled crowds, he noticed Mai Zetterling in a gleaming red mackintosh, and found time to question Cecil Beaton about his recently published photographs of the infant Prince Andrew. Among the three hundred guests, he noted the presence of Colin Wilson and Colin MacInnes (who had written the introduction to the catalogue), and Nubar Gulbenkian, testifying to the strength of Ida's Armenian connections. Champagne and white wine flowed, and Ida herself had provided caviar for her guests.

It was a frenetic event, packed with reviewers, sitters, colleagues and supporters. Even those who knew Ida's photographs well were staggered by the size of the prints and the disturbing effect of the massive grainy figures which stared out from the carefully arranged screens. No one in London had ever seen anything quite like it. Ida herself was every inch the great photographer. The slights and snubs of the past were forgotten as, dressed in black, hair swept back, she received the praise and recognition for which she had strived for so long.

The huge enlargements made for Ida by the Autotype Company for the Whitechapel exhibition. F. N. Souza, Georges Braque, and Gino Severini (left to right)

Ida and her 1960 portrait of Augustus John

Some of those whose portraits were on show were unable to attend. The sculptor Barbara Hepworth was ill, but wrote to Ida to say that she had 'heard splendid reports about the whole exhibition'.[12] Henry Moore sent his apologies, but promised to come to see the show during its first week. The historian Helmut Gernsheim (who was to become one of Ida's most invaluable supporters) avoided the party because he 'wanted to see photographs rather than people'[13] but visited the exhibition later and was much impressed by 'Ida's powerful close-ups [and by] the fact that each photograph was designed and enlarged for the space where it hung'.[14] The Whitechapel exhibition was Gernsheim's introduction to Ida's work, and after their first meeting, the two became close friends. Looking back at Ida's photography now, Gernsheim reflects:

> her portraits belong to the finest taken in Britain in the 1950s and 1960s, yet her work was too unusual and did not find the lasting appreciation it deserved. It also proved a considerable financial burden to her. Today, she would undoubtedly receive a bursary from the Arts Council, who did not accept photography as a supportable art until 1972.[15]

Many others responded to the exhibition with enthusiasm. The writer Olivia Manning, whom Ida had photographed in the mid-1950s, wrote from her home in St John's Wood:

> I felt I must tell you that the exhibition is magnificent. I am sure it will establish you in the front rank of photographers today. Some of the portraits are extremely haunting. I was particularly impressed by that of Augustus John, so wonderful and so terrible – an old man looking straight into the eyes of death.[16]

Colin MacInnes, the acerbic chronicler of metropolitan life in the fifties, was ebullient in his praise for the show: 'The exhibition is a splendour. I have never in my life seen a display of photographs that gave so strong a feeling of the *artist* who had made them, and which even succeeded in transcending the limitations of the medium and creating something wonderful and lasting.'[17]

As Ida had hoped, the reviewers flocked to the exhibition. The *Daily Worker* commented on the scarcity of photography shows in Britain, and went on to discuss the even greater rarity of a woman photographer holding a one-person show at an important public venue.[18] Winifred Carr, of the *Daily Telegraph*, interviewed Ida at home in D'Arblay Street, and predicted that photography was set to become 'the most "U" of careers' and that it would soon be 'accepted by the rarefied world of serious art'.[19] She also predicted that 'a new fashion in portraits is coming in, that of having a character study photography which is then blown-up to life-size and hung up as a mural in the sitting-room or, framed for a company boardroom'.

Elsewhere in the press, *Vogue* magazine opined that Ida's sitters seemed more like victims than clients. (The same had been said of Julia Margaret Cameron, and indeed, throughout photographic critical theory, from Cameron to Diane Arbus, women portraitists have frequently been seen as predatory.) *The Times* cautiously acknowledged that 'the photographs may be considered as works of art in themselves', thus beginning a debate that continued throughout the showing and which did much to influence opinion in the next decade.

Many reporters and reviewers noted that Ida's exhibition was the first one-person photography show to be held in a major London art gallery. Ida herself had gone to great pains to remind the press of the exhibition's uniqueness in this respect, and the claim remained as one of her standard pieces of publicity throughout the remainder of her career. When the *Guardian*'s reviewer visited the exhibition, he was struck by Ida's ability 'to underline character without dramatising it into a situation'.[20], and went on to give perceptive descriptions of the portraits of Behan, Stanley Spencer (page 139), Cecil Beaton (page 126) and Epstein (page 82). Even the populist *Reynold's News* sought Ida out to ascertain her feelings about middle-age. 'Women are so silly to worry about their wrinkles,' she told the paper's reporter on 3 April, 'they can make a face so much more interesting.' The *Observer* newspaper asked the photographer Eric de Maré to view the exhibition, thus producing one of the reviews which looked more closely at the photography than it did at the famous sitters. De Maré told readers that, 'the status of creative photographers is lower here than abroad, but it has been improving lately',[21] and drew attention both to the size of the prints and the proof they provided, 'that on rare occasions, photography can rise to the level of an art in its own right'.[22] He also mentioned Ida's use of a Rolleiflex camera, and the fact that she took only twelve shots at each sitting.

Most of the art magazines sent reviewers to the Whitechapel exhibition. Jasia Reichardt, assessing the photographs for *Arts News and Review* on 26 March, made acute and perceptive observations about Ida herself and the medium as a whole: 'The possibilities of photography have not yet been fully explored. The photographer's career has in reality been established only recently with that of the copy writer, public relations man, television producer and industrial psychologist.'

How telling it was of the post-war decline of photography that it should now, with the rise of a modern media, be seen as something new. Reichardt's views were prophetic; photographers were indeed to take their place, in the new decade, as the fashionable stars of the meritocracy. To many onlookers, Ida's exhibition, with its boldness, its scale, signalled the beginning of the revival.

Jasia Reichardt's piece in *Arts News and Review* was by far the most perceptive to emerge from the show's press coverage. She saw beyond the professionalism and the pride, which was so much of Ida's public image, to the struggle she had had since coming to London: 'Her early years in England could have been plotted on a chart with the following headings: perseverance, blundering, despair, hope and frustration.' She drew attention to Ida's predilection for 'the romantic, violent and sentimental', noting that it was 'not surprising that she feels equally at home with the disorderly surroundings of an artist's studio or the opulent interior of a stately home'. Reichardt pinpointed with accuracy one of the major thrusts of Ida's portraiture; she looked behind the celebrity portraits and saw a rich visual intellect at work, constructing stage sets out of real lives and real places, always looking for surface and pattern, for tensions and contrasts.

Another young reviewer who looked with care at Ida's exhibition prints was the writer Bernard Kops, sent by the Labour Party's *Tribune* newspaper: 'It is all here,' he wrote, 'the happiness, the sadness, the humility and conceit, the gentle, the forceful. This work recognises the objective things of life, affirms life and carries that affirmation back into reality.'[23] Kops recalled that he 'entered feeling that if photography is an art, then Ida Kar is a major artist' and that he 'left knowing that if it hadn't been art up to now, she certainly had elevated it into that position'.[24] He also observed the kind of people who were coming into the gallery to see the show: 'men in bowler hats, several workmen, a lot of old ladies, shop girls, pale clerks, intense art students and smartly dressed teenagers'.[25] The observation was an important one, for it draws attention to the fact that the exhibition was populist, entertaining and attracting wide public notice.

Most of the critics were agreed that if photography could be classed as art, then Ida Kar's photographs were worthy of the definition.[26] 'Is photography art?' became the main theme of 'The Critics' discussion of the Whitechapel show, broadcast by the BBC

The exhibition at the Whitechapel Art Gallery, 1960

on its Third Programme midway through the run of the exhibition. The BBC had brought together David Sylvester, Jacques Bruinus and Edgar Anstay to air their views on this topical subject. From the beginning of the discussion, the art establishment, represented by David Sylvester, was trenchant in its opinions: 'I do not think that photographs are ever works of art ... the artist *creates* his forms and does not select them: photography reproduces the form.'[27] Later in the programme Sylvester asserted: 'I think the essence of a painting is its absolute rightness of scale. If the scale of a photograph can be variable, I don't think that photography can be a true art.'[28]

True or false art, reproduction or creation, the public at least was prepared to believe in Ida's work. Whether or not they thought it art now hardly seems to matter. Over ten thousand people came to look at the photographs during the run of the exhibition, and thirty-five separate journals carried reviews. Although sales of works did not even begin to pay for the exhibition's costs, a surprising number of photographs priced at between fifty and one hundred pounds were sold. The Grosvenor Gallery bought portraits of Chagall and Severini, Roland Browse and Delbanco bought the photograph of Josef Herman, and the Waddington Gallery purchased Ida's study of Ivon Hitchens.

Ida Kar's Whitechapel exhibition marked a significant reversal in the hitherto declining fortunes of the medium in Britain. It proved to both the public and the establishment that photography could be bold, that it could move and delight a large audience. It showed that photography could be reviewed and appreciated in exactly the same way as painting and sculpture. Significantly, it marked the arrival of the photographer as media personality. For Ida herself, it was both a huge success and a terrible disaster. Financially, its costs crippled her for the remainder of her career. Emotionally, it presented her with a mirage of fame, a suggestion of celebrity, which was never to become a reality. Like many talented pioneers, Ida was unable to properly manage her success. She never again produced photographs of the clarity and lucidity which she had made in the 1950s. She had expanded and enlarged her photographic imagination during Britain's bleakest decade, but, as the cultural scene began to liven as the new decade progressed, her vision was darkened and obscured. In the early years of the 1960s, Ida was a celebrity. She was filmed for Pathe News, and was guest at the *Women of the Year* luncheon. By the end of the decade, she was virtually forgotten.

CHAPTER FOUR

Inheriting the party
Life and work from 1960 to 1974

'England is a strange country, whose custom it is to ignore its men of genius for as long as possible, and to denigrate them as soon as possible after their deaths.' [1]

As Ida Kar's huge enlargements were being removed carefully from the walls of the Whitechapel Art Gallery, a new era was beginning. As affluence replaced austerity, as art became fashion and fashion became all, the direction of cultural life in Britain began to alter. With the expansion of social and educational opportunities, together with the arrival of more populist art forms – rock music, photography and television all came into this category – it was no longer so necessary to venture into Soho to escape from philistinism and convention.

For those who were youthful and talented and amibitious at the beginning of the 1960s, it probably all just seemed to be in the natural order of things. For those who had clawed their way through the tough years of the post-war, the coming of better times saw some bizarre re-shuffling as the new opportunities of the decade began to emerge. Television was in its ascendant. Photography was again a fashionable occupation, with its practitioners becoming symbols of financial and social success. Fashion, too, lost much of its usage as a marker of social class and income, and became a vital expression of personal philosophies and individualism. Good or bad, misjudged and over-romanticised as it may have been, the tide of the new culture was powerful and unabating. For many of Ida's friends and associates, it was a question of sink or swim. Some found the swimming an exhilarating experience; Ida's near contemporary Cecil Beaton found himself gleefully in a new world, pub-crawling in the East End, making the acquaintance of the Rolling Stones in Tangier, being photographed by David Bailey, and noticing that 'the Beat-look is out. Dancing the Shake; no-one minding anything or anybody.'[2]

Others, who had glimpsed the enormous moral and social hypocrisies of post-war Britain, saw the coming decade, its wildness and irreverence, as an inevitable reaction to the corruption of the past. The fifties had been austere, elitist and riddled with hypocrisies, but the 1960s could be perceived as subversive and anti-authoritarian, with what one contemporary commentator called the 'ragged underground army' emerging from the 'Liverpool cellars, the docklands of Bermondsey and the narrow streets of Shoreditch'.[3] For Ida Kar, the new iconoclasm while welcome, was untimely. The photographs which she had shown to such remarkable effect at the Whitechapel were well in the vanguard of the photographic revival. Their chalky whites, harsh black and dramatic grain were the inspiration of a whole new generation of young photographers. Ida herself, however, did not become a fashionable figure. An oddly conventional character in fifties bohemia, the subsequent cultural revolution with its schema of pop and psychedelia made her appear even more out of date. In a decade which debunked, Ida still believed fervently in great men and great art. In a decade when it was fashionable to be forever young, Ida refused to rejuvenate.

Nevertheless, for her the sixties had begun on a high note. The success of the Whitechapel show had given Ida much confidence. Just three months after the exhibition had closed, she was instructing a literary agent to take a synopsis of a planned book of her photographs to Frankfurt Book Fair.[4] She hoped for a lavish production, to include a hundred photographs, and introductions by Colin MacInnes, Jean Cocteau and Henry Moore. Ida proposed to contribute full technical details about each photograph. She hoped very much for a European or American publisher for her book, and during 1960, discussed the project with both Viking of New York and Editions du Chêne in Paris. She even went so far as to suggest to Viking that plans for an American exhibition of her work were quite far advanced, although in reality, no firm proposals had yet been made. Disappointing it must have been when Viking decided not to take a chance with 'the publication in book form of 100 photographs by a photographer as yet unknown in this country'[5] and the prospective French publisher likewise rejected the idea because there were so few portraits in Ida's collection of artists and writers well known in France.

For Ida, an internationally distributed book of her photographs would have opened up completely fresh areas of interest, activity and income. Usually so undaunted by difficulties, the failure of this first project dampened Ida's enthusiasm for publishing. Her 1960 book proposal was her last and only approach to either British or American publishers.

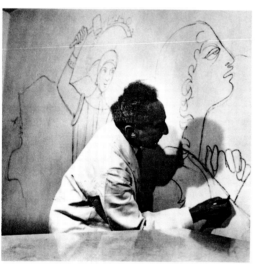

Jean Cocteau, France, early 1950s

As the 1960s began, Ida was more in need of both effective promotion and good advice than ever before. In the fifties her imagination had been at its most potent, her energy enormous, her vision sharp and clear and radical. Behind the façade of eccentricity and extravagance which intrigued and entertained her sitters was an intelligence which probed skilfully into the vanities, preoccupations and obsessions of her sitters. After the Whitechapel exhibition, she found that her creativity was severely diminished. Although she attempted to continue her series of photographs of British cultural leaders by photographing a rather diverse set of people (including the actor Jack Hawkins and the publisher Hamish Hamilton), the pictures which emerged had none of the vitality and acuteness of the work which she had produced in the 1950s. It was as if the recognition which she had so longed for had stifled the very impulses which had originally earned her fame and praise.

Uninspired as she may have felt after the Whitechapel project, Ida soon embarked on another major photographic enterprise.

By the summer of 1960, she was planning a second trip to the Soviet Union. She visited Armenia in November, and divided her time between photography and visits to her father, who was recently widowed. She grieved for her surviving parent: 'He is a poor devil of an old man. Lonely and unhappy, and he cannot be alone. I hope he will come out of the hospital and get married.'[6] Unhappy as she was for her father, and as impatient as she became with the friends and relatives who surrounded him – 'Armenia is a horrible place, so much gossip. They make me want to vomit'[7] – she nevertheless set herself a full programme of photographic work. She was so proud of her efforts that she offered enthusiastic advice to friends back at home: 'If Kasmin wants to make money he must get up at 9.30 in the morning and have breakfast with me and work every day from 9 to 11 systematically.'[8] She assured Victor that she would be able to produce 'a sensational exhibition' from the film which she had taken, in spite of the delays which she felt had been caused by the ponderous Armenian bureaucracy: 'I am trying to work as hard as I can, but do very little. So many permissions are necessary for everything, and the time passes in exhausting telephone calls.'[9]

From Armenia she travelled to Moscow, where she photographed the staff of the British Embassy, producing a set of pictures which was subsequently published in the *Sunday Express* in the following year. Apart from this convivial project, her stay in Moscow was a lonely one. She spent her evenings going alone to the theatre and the cinema, and despaired of the Moscow weather which instead of producing picturesque snow, was dark and rainy.

John Cox, assistant and companion, 1950s

Attending a private view, London, early 1960s

Back in Soho, the new year brought some significant changes. Both Kasmin and Ida's assistant/companion, John Cox, had finally ceased to work for her. Tempestuous and frequently uneasy as her relationship had been with these two men, both had become vital pillars of support for her and for her photography. Change became even more evident in the spring of 1961, when Gallery One moved to new premises in North Audley Street in Mayfair. At the opening party, for a one-man show by Rufino Tamayo, Ida seemed oddly out of date and conservative. 'Only one woman wore a hat,' commented the *Evening Standard* reporter acidly, 'Ida Kar should go to Ascot.'[1]

If things were changing with an alarming rapidity in photography, then the art world seemed to be even more volatile. Those who had established small innovative galleries in the post-war cultural desert saw similar enterprises multiply all over London. 'Eight years ago,' wrote Neville Wallis in the *Observer*, 'there were barely a dozen modern art galleries in the West End. Today, seventy galleries are exhibiting contemporary art from Soho through Mayfair to Knightsbridge.'[11]

Throughout 1961, Ida's photography remained stagnant. The old sureness of vision had, for the time being, deserted her. Hamish Hamilton, while congratulating Ida on 'making me look human in one out of the three photographs' advised that 'the others should please be destroyed and forgotten'.[12]

By the end of the year, Ida was travelling in Europe again, this time to the South of France. She hoped to organise a portrait sitting with Picasso, and was also meeting up with Madame Léger, widow of the celebrated French artist, to arrange a loan of paintings for Gallery One. The trip exhausted her, she felt the intense heat and she was too short of money to enjoy the luxuries of the Riviera. Her journey home by train from Cannes was enlivened by her meeting with an Englishwoman of Russian extraction. Ida was intrigued to learn, during the course of their conversation, that Natalie Preston's nineteen-year-old daughter was an enthusiastic student of photography, studying at the Regent Street Polytechnic. A meeting between Ida and the young Julieta Preston was swiftly arranged:

I went to see her – she was such an electric character that I was totally captivated the minute I met her. I thought she was the most extraordinary person and clearly a brilliant photographer. I was halfway through my course at the Poly, I'd only been there for eighteen months, and Ida, in her typical way, said, 'I've got a wonderful plan for you – come and work for me and I'll teach you everything you need to know.'[13]

It was a reflection both of Ida's improved status and her perennial lack of money that the young people who, up to now, had been assistants, were now 'pupils'. Julieta Preston was Ida's first pupil, and boarded with Ida and Victor, first at D'Arblay Street and later at Stanhope Place, near Hyde Park. For Ida, the relationship was an important one. Julieta became assistant, pupil and companion. Ida developed a strong, almost maternal affection for this young woman. She had always been well disposed towards other women, although she had no close women friends, and as the sixties progressed, she became increasingly interested in women's issues, and her sympathy with feminism grew. Julieta Preston's time with Ida was a combination of photography and domesticity:

> I developed all her films. And printed all the contact sheets. I developed all her stuff when she got back from Russia. I answered the telephone and dealt with people, and some of the time I was just a companion, going with her to things. She'd suddenly decide we'd go out for a meal or something, or we'd go shopping. Sometimes she'd spend the whole day cooking and I would help her. Days would go by and we wouldn't do anything connected with photography. Lots of people came round. Victor and Ida had this curious love-hate relationship. He had his parties at Gallery One, we always went to those . . . and he gave outrageous parties, in terms of the people he invited and the clothes they turned up in. It was a whole new world to me. It was a maze of people. We often used to go to exhibitions together – we'd go to a succession of first nights, they were all the rage then. Victor was always sweeping us off to first nights.[14]

Full and interesting as Ida's life was, it was becoming obvious to those close to her that she was experiencing greater and greater difficulty in dealing with her professional life. What had been a tempestuous and autocratic manner in the fifties was emerging now as an aggressive eccentricity. Her major projects were invariably accompanied by storms and upsets which had begun to go beyond the bounds of acceptable behaviour. After a time, her reputation invariably began to precede her, and many planned projects were never realised. To many potential clients and gallery curators, she was a difficult woman, and better avoided. She was unfortunate in that she no longer had people around her who could conceal or soften her manner and attitude to the outside world. Utterly convinced too of the worth of her photography and of her own talents, she no longer saw any need to promote herself or her work. Even more problematic was her seeming inability to expand and strengthen her photography; she was no longer producing the kind of portraiture which had established her so firmly as one of the leading documentarists of British cultural life, nor had she found any new and vital direction in which to progress.

However, at the beginning of 1962, the future seemed full of promise. Ida immersed herself in the complex arrangements for her forthcoming exhibition at Moscow's House of Friendship. She managed inevitably to ruffle some diplomatic feathers on the way: 'Things in Moscow do not work as you seem to think,'[15] wrote the Ambassador's wife Lady Roberts with some asperity, following Ida's attempts to combine her own complicated exhibition negotiations with a well-meaning attempt to secure a Moscow show for her old Gallery One friend, F. N. Souza.

The exhibition re-awakened press interest in Ida's work, although inevitably not everyone responded enthusiastically to her portraits: 'How odd', asked an irate Bristol reader of the *British Journal of Photography*, 'must a photograph be before it is considered artistic?'[16] Ida had become highly skilled at organising her own publicity, and in dealing with the press. She liked to be interviewed, and her frank and generous nature made the welcome which she gave to journalists and reviewers an obviously genuine one. In the publicity material which she released before the Moscow exhibition, she dwelt less on the artistic content of the show than on its size, its planned journey to the Soviety Union and its prospective celebrity visitors: 'Miss Kar's exhibition is probably the biggest cargo of photographs ever sent to Moscow. There are 76 large scale photographs, some of them six feet high. Owing to their size, the photographs are being flown by special aircraft to Moscow.[17] She also announced with pride that the opening party at the House of Friendship would be attended not only by the British, French and American ambassadors, but also by the cosmonaut Yuri Gagarin and the composer Shostakovitch.

By the end of February, Ida reported to Victor, who was abroad: 'we have continuous interviews and receptions'.[18] She also warned him: 'I get up every morning at five o'clock and work until nine at night. I do not wish to be disturbed after nine and during that time I work hecticly (sic) and cannot accept any interruption which has not been previously fixed.'[19] More good news seemed imminent in the prospect of a grant from the wealthy Gulbenkian Foundation. She hoped for an award which would fund her for the next five years, and she also planned to offer for purchase to the nation all

At the Moscow Exhibition, 1962. Ida's portrait of Bernard Kops and his family is in the background, (right)

her exhibition photographs for 'British propaganda and educational purposes in the provinces' for a suggested price of £10,000. Her optimism was short-lived, as neither plan came to fruition, and she found herself again in the by now familiar position of facing the expenses of a major exhibition with no promise of support, and scanty financial resources of her own.

The press did not hesitate to write about her latest venture. She advised the readers of the *Daily Worker*:

> Stick with one camera. Learn it backwards. So as you don't have to think of techniques and mechanics. I exploit my materials to their full limit. This doesn't mean falling for every brand of developer, every fresh batch of printing papers, which spill out from the manufacturers.[20]

On being asked by *Queen* magazine why she photographed so few women, she replied roundly, 'I photograph famous people, and famous people are mainly men. Beauties leave me cold.' Most satisfying of all however was the publication of an article entitled 'Artist with a Camera', in the February edition of the fine arts magazine *Studio*. Brian Robbins' moody portrait of Ida was used on the cover, and seven of her own photographs of artists (including Stanley Spencer, Epstein and L. S. Lowry) were printed in a major feature about her work. For Ida, who by 1962, must have been a little weary of the old debate about whether photography was or was not art, the calm, considered praise of *Studio* must have been welcome, even if long overdue:

> So far has representational art fled from contemporary practice that it is left to the artist-photographer to prove that the real truth lies in allowing the subject to speak for itself, choosing with patience and the intuitive selection of light the moment when the shutter falls and reality is crystallised, distilled and preserved in one flat image.[21]

Studio asked its readers to:

> Look at her photographs reproduced on the six pages here. Composition is at its most complete when one can read the range of tone from deadest of white to silky ebony black. In the faces of artists we know, we see the veritable image of art that they would all endorse to be there: making by her design the essence, not merely the reflection of the isolated reality.[22]

It was a wonderful prelude to the Moscow exhibition. At one end of the publishing spectrum, serious art magazines discussed her work just as they would a painter's, at the other, she was hailed as a personality and she became the tenth woman to be included in the *Evening Standard*'s 'Women of Impact' series. The *Standard*'s reporter, Shirley Lord, described her thus:

> Visually, she will always make impact – not only because of the black astrakhan cossack hat she likes to wear even on hot summer days, or because of the black stockings or the steady burning glances from her dark eyes. Ida surges into places – as she surges into my office there is a tendency for my secretary to move towards her desk, the mental vibration she causes in so small a space is unavoidably stirring.[23]

Ida, by then in her fifty-fourth year, had already begun to equivocate about her true age. She would allow the *Standard* to say only that she was 'over forty'. It perhaps added to her fear of ageing that most of her friends and colleagues were appreciably younger than herself. She had always thrived on the company of young people, but her predilection for youth had distinct disadvantages, making her acutely aware of her own advancing age. In many ways, Ida had never truly grown up, she had rarely if ever been truly financially self-sufficient, she relied heavily on others for emotional and professional support, she had none of the family responsibilities which were being borne by many of her contemporaries. Free as her way of life may have made her to pursue her work, to travel at home and abroad, it also served increasingly to imprison her in her own isolation.

During these years, Ida built up a façade with which to deceive the world. Bright, engaging, imperious, ageless, she became like a character from fiction, from the kind of novel which deals brilliantly with surface and effect, but which fails to uncover real motives, and real lives. In her late middle age, Ida had begun to play the part of Ida with an eerie accuracy. The Moscow exhibition of 1962 was her last real attempt to establish herself as a photography superstar. The photographs taken of her during the course of the show and which she brought back from the USSR and mounted in her press-cuttings album were images which correspond entirely to her self-view. In one, she poses in front of the entrance to the House of Friendship, wearing leather boots, belted leather coat and carrying camera bag and print portfolio. She is intrepid and in control. In others, taken inside the exhibition hall, she is by turn

On the steps of the House of Friendship, Moscow, 1957. The posters for the exhibition can be seen behind Ida

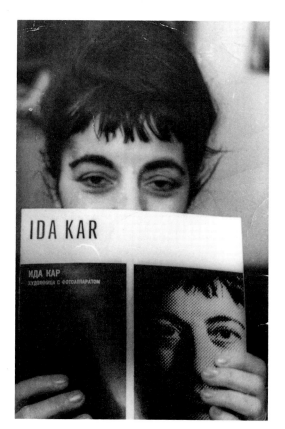

The catalogue for the Moscow Exhibition, 1962

With the Russian photographer Paola, Moscow, 1962.
(*Private collection*)

glamorous, reflective and sternly intellectual.

So important for Ida was the spectacle of an exhibition, and her own position at the centre of it, that her continued inability to produce new work must have been increasingly alarming. Many of her portraits would soon be out of date, some of those whom she had photographed in the fifties were no longer voguish figures. The old work could not be continually re-shown, and to carry on her successful series of exhibitions, she had to begin to produce innovative new work. All around her in London, dramatic, uncompromising portraits by a variety of young photographers of celebrities in art, literature, music and the media had begun to be published in the glossy magazines. Her own application to the *Sunday Times* to take the place of the portraitist Douglas Glass was not successful. She had hoped desperately for the position, for its guaranteed salary and regular exposure of work, and the rejection was yet another indication that her career was failing to advance.

Nevertheless, the success of the Moscow exhibition, which opened in April at the House of Friendship, was greatly reassuring. The Soviet press reviewed the show generously, and esteemed Russian writers and artists testified to their respect for her work. The writer Leonid Leonov was courtly in his praise:

Photography today has become a rather complex art, especially now that the requisite processes and materials are seemingly available to all. It is a wonderful creation of modern civilisation, in which is united the knowledge of the chemist, the genius of the lens expert, the labour of the workman and all the intricate ingenuity of industrial production. But success in this field is reached only when the wonderful lens becomes the eye of the sensitive and observing artist. It is precisely because of this that it is so difficult to single the photographer out from the crowd, but you have succeeded in creating a most interesting gallery of contemporaries – in your own country and in other lands.[24]

The sculptor Nicolas Tomsky was as fulsome when he reviewed Ida's exhibition for an English language publication in Moscow, and recalled:

When she visited my studio, I was able to see her at work. She is lively, energetic and quickly finds her bearings in any situation. Not more than five minutes were required to establish an artistic and creative contact between us. Where does such talent spring from? I believe it is born from an ardent love of Art, in whose

Cutting the tape to open the exhibition at the House of Friendship, Moscow, 1962

atmosphere the whole of Ida Kar's life is spent. This love both sharpens and refines the senses. Not for nothing do they say that love produces miracles. It is sufficient to see her gallery of artists to become convinced of this.[25]

For Ida, it must have seemed a fitting tribute from another artist.

By the end of March, Ida was in Moscow to oversee the hanging of her photographs. In a letter home, she described the procedure in some detail, telling Victor that 'the hanging started with two expert workmen, an artistic adviser and myself' and explaining to him at some length how a large information plaque was removed to allow her photographs an uninterrupted run down a long corridor. The final hanging was to her satisfaction, and she thought the completed exhibition 'simply magnificent'.[26]

Impressive as the show undoubtedly was, containing much of Ida's best work from the fifties as well as photographs made recently in the USSR, the troublesome question remained as to who was to pay for it all. In the flurry of organising the exhibition, no firm agreement had been arrived at about who should meet the project's costs. From Moscow she wrote to Victor: 'the only thing I have not succeeded in is either to get the Soviets to pay for the cost of the plane or the catalogues, or to allow me to sell them. I have not abandoned the idea of getting permission, and I attack them from right and left. I have gone as far as saying they have no heart.'[27] In England she had written in some desperation to a potential sponsor[28] that, although she had firmly believed that the Great Britain–USSR Society had promised to cover her costs, 'Now they told me they only sponsor me for the sum of 200 pounds.' She calculated that 'the transport alone is beyond that sum, and there are various expenses such as translation of my catalogue, which is being done this weekend, etc. etc'.

She still had debts of over £1,000 from the Whitechapel show, and was horrified at the prospect of incurring more. She wrote:

Can you tell me if I can come under an Arts Council grant as soon as possible to assist me and to allow me to continue the work I have started in 1953 and to be able to have the exhibition in Moscow and arrange another exhibition, this time at the New York Museum of Modern Art, without being worried and harassed by debts.[29]

How, when and by whom the project was finally paid for remains unclear, but the show itself was a resounding success, and Ida was buoyant again. After spending a few days with her father in Erevan and resting in Paris at the home of Marie-Thérèse Lelio, she returned home to London: 'I certainly wish you to see that the press meets me at Victoria Station this time,' she wrote to Victor, and confided to him that she longed to be back: 'There is nowhere as good as your own home they say. Also I rather miss my own cooking ... Back from Erevan, I found your most loving letter. How can I resist your natural charm and not write to you?'[30]

As usual, the months which followed the exhibition were anti-climactic. After the bustle and excitement of the Moscow project, Ida found little in London to interest or inspire her. She hoped that she might be invited to take part in one of the new television arts programmes but the producers could find no place for her in their schedules. Her friend Ivon Hitchens wrote to reassure her:

> There is always the horrible gap after any show which is partly reaction and partly actual exhaustion, and partly because one doesn't know where one is going to start again – how or when. Gradually one slips into it once more – and then something fires your imagination – and 'hey presto' – one is in full swing again. I think you will find that happens.[31]

The spark which re-ignited Ida's imagination came in the end from an unlikely source. 'Since I returned from Moscow I was very depressed,' she wrote to Heinrich Heidersberger. 'I hated my work, therefore myself, and did not care whether I was alive or dead. Then the miracle happened, a new interest and opportunity, animal photography.'[32] At the beginning of 1963, a sister journal for the popular *Knowledge* magazine was launched. Entitled *Animals*, and edited by John Chancellor, Ida was invited to produce photographs for it on a regular basis. It was indeed a startling departure for a photographer who had no obvious interest in the natural world, and who knew so little about animals that even at the height of her involvement with the magazine she admitted that she very rarely knew what any of her subjects were called. Few of her friends and colleagues felt able to give her their full support: 'I *do* wish you success,' wrote Douglas Glass, 'but there is very little "reflected glory" in photographing animals. It *does* seem a waste of your excellent talent for humans. I hope it pays at least.'[33]

The journalist Roger Hill, writing for the *Evening Standard*, accompanied Ida on one of her trips to London Zoo, and recorded how, after both had taken flight from an angry sea-lion, Ida had confided: 'There are a few more people I want to photograph –

In the company of animals: Ida photographing a panda at London Zoo, 1963

Khrushchev, the Queen, Picasso, Edith Sitwell and a few more faces I may find interesting. But now I can devote my time to my animals.'[34] Julieta Preston, who frequently accompanied Ida on her many visits to zoos, was aware that there was little enthusiasm for Ida's new project:

> I don't think people were ever very interested in the animal photographs – she was very interested in promoting them, but I felt that people felt that she'd peaked. In my view, the animal photography was a diversion, they were lovely, but they weren't special, like the portraits of people. In some ways I think, taking the animals was an escape. Because she just found dealing with people so difficult.[35]

Pursued by a chimpanzee at Cologne Zoo, 1963

Ida's animal photography certainly failed to attract the kind of attention which had been paid to her portraits of artists and writers. However, she carried out her new work with interest and much diligence. As the years passed, she became increasingly intrigued by zoo animals, returning to London Zoo until the late 1960s, long after her work for *Animals* magazine had ceased. Ida's animal photography is distinguished more by its flawless technique than by its artistry. It also has a pathos which is difficult to define. Whatever its strengths and weaknesses, it did at least provide Ida with some photographic direction at a time when she was at her least inspired.

Throughout the first half of the sixties she continued to exhibit work from the fifties and her newer animal portraits. Her next major show was held at Birmingham's City Museum and Art Gallery in May 1963. The prospect of this new exhibition at an important regional centre gave her renewed energies, as she explained to Heinrich Heidersberger, a few weeks before the show was due to open:

> Since Christmas I have been working over ten hours a day and the last two months I have been getting up at 5 o'clock in the morning and stopping work at 10 o'clock at night. The reason for all this is the weekly magazine which I am contributing to and my forthcoming exhibition at the Birmingham Museum. The exhibition . . . is a very big thing and a very unusual one. Some of the photographs you have seen before in black and white. Added to them are forty new ones up to six feet high which will be on the walls, while animal transparencies in colour up to 20″ × 24″ illuminated from the back will be on stands.[36]

The photographer and the photographed: Ida at London Zoo, early 1960s

As well as showing in Birmingham, Ida was participating in the *Nature Week* activities in London and provided eight of her colour transparencies for exhibition during the third week of May. That spring, however, it seemed as if all the doubts and depression of the previous year had vanished. Whatever problems there had been about the costs of the Moscow show seemed to have been resolved. She was showing work in both London and Birmingham, and had plans, albeit vague ones, to exhibit in the United States and in France.

Opportunities to lecture and teach were fairly frequent, and ranged from an appearance at a Foyle's Literary Luncheon to a talk in July to the Photographic Club at Wandsworth Prison. She was a good speaker, full of humour and anecdote, and at the same time highly informative about the art and technique of portrait photography.

All other activities were put aside for a time as Ida prepared her work for shipment to Birmingham's City Art Gallery and Museum. Entitled *Ida Kar – Artist with a Camera*, the show was given much prominence by its organisers. The Museum issued an elegant private view card and publicity leaflet, and invited the public to attend a Luncheon Hour Lecture, to be given by Ida on 23 May. Apart from the near loss and subsequent late arrival of the catalogues from London, the exhibition went smoothly. It was based very much on the Whitechapel show, with the same dramatic enlargements and many of her best-liked portraits from the fifties, including her studies of Braque, Brendan Behan and John Rothenstein. Although the press coverage was much less than she would have expected in London, the regional newspapers sent reviewers and photographers to the show. The *Birmingham Post*'s photographer posed Ida and Julieta Preston in front of her famous portrait of the ageing Augustus John, and the *Evening Mail and Despatch*[37] showed Ida kneeling between her study of Le Corbusier (mis-named in the newspaper as Léger) and an outsize colour transparency of a porcupine.

The first week of the exhibition also saw the sale of Ida's 'Portrait of a Spanish Painter', and the event was surprising enough for the local paper to headline a piece about the exhibition 'Photograph sold for Sixty Guineas'. There was little serious reviewing of the exhibition. Although the art critic of the *Birmingham Post* attempted to revive the old 'Is Photography Art?' debate, and at the same time warned his public that 'photographers are potentially worse bores than painters', he conceded that Ida's photographs were 'exceptional and free of gimmicks'.[38]

In the kitchen at Stanhope Place, early 1960s
Photograph by John Morris

Cuba, 1964

Birmingham was Ida's first real experience of the regions, and she was struck by the city's vitality and cultural awareness. She became friendly with John Morris, a serious amateur photographer living in the city, and gave him much assistance in mounting an exhibition of his own work at the Midland Arts Centre. Five years later, in 1968, Ida herself exhibited at the Arts Centre, in the company of Bill Brandt, the editor and photographer Bill Jay, and two of her pupils, Julieta Preston and John Couzins. It was obvious that Ida was well suited to enthusiastic participation in the coming revival of creative photography, as she remarked to a Birmingham reporter: 'I am fifty-five, but I have the vitality of a twenty-five-year-old. I am sure I shall never feel too old to do what I want.'[39]

The summer of 1963 brought more changes. After over a decade in the friendly, bohemian cosmopolitanism of Soho, Ida and Victor left D'Arblay Street. From that time until their eventual separation, they lived in a succession of Mayfair flats. For a time, they lived in Stanhope Place, a small street just across the Bayswater Road from Hyde Park. Ida's friend John Morris, who maintained contact with both her and Victor until the mid-1960s, remembers visiting them in a red brick apartment building in Mount Street. Their last Mayfair home was in a mews house in Rex Place, just behind the Dorchester Hotel. The domestic routine went on much as usual, with Ida making shopping trips to her favourite and familiar Soho shops and markets. More fundamental an alteration to their lives was the closure of Gallery One, in the summer of 1963. After more than ten years as the alternative centre of the London art world, the gallery, with its lively programme, its controversial choices, its convivial opening parties, had finally gone. Gone too, by the end of the year, was Ida's post with *Animals* magazine. Much bitterness obviously surrounded her departure, and in an angry letter to John Chancellor, she stressed her professionalism, the widespread admiration for her work among the photographic community and the general low regard in which other *Animals* employees were held by the outside world. Her passionate defence of herself and her work had little obvious effect, for by November, Helmut Gernsheim, back in London for a short stay, was writing to sympathise with her for 'the disappointments you experienced through the lack of orders for your portraits and the discontinuation of your work for *Animals*'.[40]

Some of the gloom and depression was dispelled by Ida's delighted receipt of an unexpected invitation from the Government of Cuba to attend the 1964 celebration of the Cuban Revolution in Havana. In January she boarded the aircraft which was to take her for a

Dancing in Cuba with one of her government drivers, 1964

five-week visit to the island. On arrival in Havana, she found that while she was expected to portray Cuba's leading writers and artists, she had much freedom, and, photographically, her greatest stimulation came from documenting street life in Havana. Ida's Cuban photographs were the best photojournalism of her career. Her unposed documentary of young Cuban women strolling the streets were the most joyful pictures she had taken since the mid-1950s. She was impressed and exhilarated by Cuban society, and moved by the Cubans' pride in their revolution. As she explored Havana, she photographed both the well-known and the ordinary people. A photograph of a young woman playing with her baby in a quiet sun-drenched doorway co-exists with a packed crowd scene, shot from above, and these city portraits stand as counterpoints to her many photographs of rural life and landscape. Snapshots taken of Ida herself while visiting Cuba show her as alert and energetic as ever. In these mementoes, which she carefully mounted in her press book, she stands on a car bonnet to capture landscape shots wearing her familiar Russian hat, samples food from a street stall and enjoys an impromptu waltz in a field with one of her drivers. Ida was pleased with the photographs she had produced in Cuba and had soon arranged an exhibition. On 9 February 1965, her *Cuba* show opened for a period of seven days at Hamiltons Gallery in St George Street, just off Hanover Square. The exhibition was then transferred to Stepney Central Library in the East End, for a further fortnight.

The critics were divided about Ida's Cuban photographs. The *British Journal of Photography*'s Bob Collins found more to say about Ida (and perhaps his own lurking fears of powerful women) than he did about the photographs: 'Meeting Ida Kar for the first time is a little like turning a sharp corner and finding oneself staring down the barrel of a seventeenth-century cannon with a smoking fuse.'[41] He found that by comparison, the exhibition paled into insignificance:

If one experiences a slight sense of disappointment, it is probably because the exhibition must be balanced inevitably against the vitality and formidable personality herself – and in consequence, it is more in her shadow than above it. In fact, taken print by print, few if any of the exhibits merit more than a moment's pause and only then because one knows they are the work of Ida Kar.[42]

Fortunately for Ida, the *British Journal* saw fit to offset this somewhat unorthodox method of art criticism (comparing the works on show to the temperament of their author was, even twenty

Speaking in defence of prostitutes at Speaker's Corner, Hyde Park, London, late 1950s

years ago, an unusual method of reviewing an exhibition of photographs) with a more careful and sensitive piece by the photographer Peggy Delius, who considered Ida's Cuban documentary to be:

> Fresh and strong, without preconceived ideas but in sympathy with her chosen subject, she brings with her present exhibition something new – a documentary quality tinged with a mixture, cool, remote yet full of burning observation. Clearly the emergence of the new Cuba has touched her creative ability profoundly.[43]

At the private view, Ida was elated, as Mark Gerson recalled: 'I was there that evening, Ida was in full flow, the television people were there and she rushed off to an interview. It was "darlings" to everybody. She was on an absolute high.'[44]

During the mid-1960s, Ida's career, once so precarious, seemed to be expanding. Serious interest in her work was at last being shown by museums both in this country and abroad. Carol Hogben, of the Victoria and Albert, arranged for the purchase of sixteen of her portraits of artists for possible use as a travelling exhibition. Even more welcome was the purchase (arranged by the indefatigable Helmut Gernsheim) of a hundred of the Whitechapel exhibition prints by the University of Texas, which also, in the course of time, acquired Gernsheim's own large photographic collection.

By the mid-1960s, however, Ida had begun to show signs of grave psychological disturbance. She developed particular obsessions, some of which centred around her marriage and her sexuality, while others led her to believe that she was being poisoned and persecuted by the agents of fascism. She veered between deep depression and manic excitement. Formerly so adept at handling the press, giving them just the right mixture of personal and professional information, Ida began to give interviews which revealed the extent of her paranoia and her obsession with Victor, her marriage and the past. To the reporter Llew Gardner, Ida confided that she had separated from Victor, although at the same time insisting that 'We are not separated. We have taken different houses. We started in the same bed, then we had separate beds. Then separate rooms, separate floors, now different houses.'[45] She was expansive about her dislike for Englishmen: 'They are very phlegmatic. It is because their mothers love them so possessively. Really the mothers believe that they are the wives. That is why there are so many homosexuals.' She spoke about her 'ideal man' – 'I like a normal man and a voluptuous man, an intelligent man. I don't want any more to be worshipped. I want to worship the man. But the trouble is the men who are my age are happily married . . . or they do not seem as virile as I am . . .' 'The only luxury I have ever had in my life,' she reflected, 'is a man to myself. No jewels, no furs. Nothing. Just a man to myself.'[46]

As the interview progressed, Ida's statements became more and more bizarre: 'I have been poisoned since Christmas,' she asserted. 'Now I am allergic to restaurants. I get puffed up. All my face gets blue. I feel terrible.'[47] Seeing the published interview, Ida obviously regretted the forthrightness of some of her statements, and within a few days she had sent a letter to the editor which modified some of her opinions. But in a subsequent newspaper interview with Taya Zinkin, Ida was even more outspoken:

I am a force! I am superhuman! That is why I must find myself through work. I have no children, and no man is BIG enough for me . . . Artists should never marry. Marriage is a habit, a routine. To wake up in the same bed all one's life with the same man, how terrible. One must fall in love, one cannot stay in love. The sink! When I think of the year I wasted by the sink! Victor complained that I am obsessed by photography. But, if one is an artist, one cannot control this obsession with one's work. I am truly dedicated.[48]

Commissioned to photograph her interviewer, Ida began by telling Zinkin: 'You have lovely hair, but your neck is short and you are fat. Don't wear chokers. I shall try and hide your neck.' Zinkin found the session

an extraordinary experience. I . . . became suddenly important, larger than life, the eye of the storm . . . she became the X-ray of my ego. I, usually so camera-shy because so unphotogenic, suddenly felt beautiful . . . I was still me, but a me of whom Ida Kar had taken charge in order to reveal me, good as well as bad. When it was all over, I felt deprived.[49]

Asked how she achieved this powerful response from her sitter, Ida replied with some drama: 'This is because I am a force. I project my self-confidence and my overwhelming love of the subject.'[50]

Drawn too into the eye of Ida's storm in the late 1960s was the young John Couzins, a photography student who replied to Ida's advertisement for pupils in the *British Journal of Photography* in 1967:

Victor Musgrave, nd.

At London Zoo, early 1960s

I was finding my feet, the advertisement intrigued me. I was even more intrigued when I met her. She had this very strong personality, and when I saw her work, it was quite staggering. In the end there were six of us pupils. She really liked to have all these young people around.[51]

By the time that Ida was advertising for her pupils, she and Victor had moved into a house which had been acquired for them at No. 16 Rex Place by an old friend and supporter of Victor's. Comfortable and roomy, it allowed for a communal sitting room, a basement kitchen and was spacious enough for Victor and Ida to live independently of each other on the first and second floors.

It wasn't long before Ida's new helpers realised that her photography was by then almost non-existent. Sometimes she and John Couzins would walk round to Mark Gerson's studio to take a few rolls of film to be developed, and occasionally Ida would order one or two new prints from the Replicard company. She photographed Arthur Koestler in Hampstead and, in the company of John Couzins, went to London Zoo to portray her favourite orang-utans, where her young pupil was struck by the rapport between Ida and the animals. As far as John Couzins was concerned: 'Pupil was a very loose term. I was a gopher of some description. I turned up there one day and nothing really occurred. I just got sucked into this incredible event.'[52]

The new pop culture was a source of much fascination for Ida. Neither she nor Victor, even in their middle age, had ever settled for the conventional. They looked constantly to the future rather than to the past. With John Couzins, Ida made an impromptu call on the Beatles at the Apple building in nearby Wigmore Street, and although she and Couzins travelled up in the lift with John Lennon and George Harrison, she was disappointed when she was unable to arrange a portrait sitting. Even more intriguing for those around her was her relationship with the Japanese performance artist Yoko Ono, who became a regular visitor to Rex Place and who collaborated with Victor on the making of an avant-garde film. Although incompatible, 'Ida and Yoko were competitors',[53] the two women became relatively close, to the point that:

Yoko rang up one day and asked to speak to Ida. When Ida put the phone down, she said, 'That was Yoko: she said "I have no more worries, I have just met a millionaire." ' And of course, that turned out to be John Lennon.[54]

Equally exciting was a visit to the distinguished British photographer Bill Brandt, then living in Notting Hill, and the everyday routine was further enlivened by opening parties at the London galleries where many of Ida's and Victor's friends congregated.

By 1968, it had become evident that the photographic revival was well under way in London. The demand for innovative photography in all areas, and particularly in fashion and advertising, provided enormous opportunities for young people entering the medium. It was obvious that an apprenticeship with Ida, who taught her pupils much about life but very little about photography, was not an ideal route to a successful career within the revived medium. By the end of the year, all of Ida's pupils had departed, and as John Couzins recalled:

> She was doing very little work. It came to a point when I wondered what I was doing there. But you get sucked into a personality like Ida's – sometimes it was very draining. She sucked the oxygen out of the air ... But it was also very enjoyable ... It was crazy, like hallucination without the drugs.[55]

Even Ida's forcefulness and the genuine affection and loyalty which Ida and Victor felt for each other could not now hold their marriage together. The strain caused by her illness on the already precarious marriage proved finally to be too great. By the end of 1969, Victor and Ida had left Rex Place and had begun a separation which lasted for the rest of Ida's lifetime. Victor made a complete break with London and Ida left Mayfair to stay with friends in Kilburn. For Ida, this final separation was a disaster. Despite her pride in her own independence, Victor had been a vital figure in her life. For years she had relied upon him, not only for the comforts of love and friendship, but also for financial support. Complain as she might about his lifestyle and fond as she undoubtedly was of the younger men with whom she had had relationships throughout the preceding years, Victor was the only real stability in Ida's increasingly uneasy world. With the worsening of her mental breakdowns, the fragile threads of mutual support and companionship which held this particular relationship together, had finally snapped. In parting from Victor, Ida had lost not only her companion of the last two decades, but also the friendly contact with the outside world which Victor had so effortlessly maintained. Almost universally liked and admired, he had attracted a wide circle of friends and associates, a circle which Ida could join or remain separate from as she wished. With the separation, that circle became much smaller. With his quietness, his discretion and his charm, Victor had been the ideal counterpoint for Ida's often overwhelming vivacity.

The separation made Ida increasingly anxious to take up photography again. She bitterly regretted the time she had spent over the years in domestic tasks, and spoke to friends about her new freedom to work and to expand her photography. But the fragile edifice had finally collapsed. She had very little work, no money except for the monthly allowance now sent to her by her brother in the United States, and almost no one to give her the support which she so desperately needed. Her troubles escalated when her illness led her into bizarre adventures, which included sleeping overnight in the deserted Lords Cricket ground, and hiring a chauffeur-driven car for a manic shopping spree in the West End, an episode which led to her eventual arrest and hospitalisation. Between stays in hospital, she could be as engaging and energetic as ever, but, alone in London for the first time in twenty years, her existence became increasingly precarious.

From the late sixties until her death in 1974 her life assumed a dismal pattern of breakdown and recovery, interspersed with moves from one shabby bedsitter to another. During the late sixties and early seventies, she moved from Mayfair to Kilburn, and back down to Bayswater, carrying with her her precious boxes of negatives and her photographic equipment. When she moved house, she often failed to tell her friends where she had gone, and there are periods in which she seems to have made no contact with those who might have assisted and supported her. Sometimes, assailed by a chronic shortage of money, she would abandon her pride and ask for money at the West End galleries where she had once been a welcome party guest. Most visitors to Ida's Bayswater flats (the first in Palace Gardens Terrace and the last at Inverness Terrace) were shocked by their bareness and lack of comfort. At Inverness Terrace, the glass roof leaked at every rainfall, and although, in the last year of her life, she had asked a building contractor to estimate the cost of its repair, the flat remained damp and cheerless throughout her occupancy.

Uncomfortable and disturbing as it all was, old friends still came to talk and to eat with her, and would hear of her latest plans for ambitious new projects. She was making tape-recordings in preparation for the writing of her autobiography[56], and, not long before her death, told Mark Gerson that she had found an exciting new model for a planned series of nudes. (During the last year of her life Ida was still actively involved with photography. In

September, she sent out three rolls of film to her West London processor, while in November, she commissioned Replicard in Highgate to mount three enlargements of zoo animals.) When she met her old friend Bill Hopkins (who had boarded at Litchfield Street in the fifties) outside on the street, and invited him back to her flat, he was much moved by her changed circumstances:

> She took me into this house. She had a couple of rooms on the ground floor, and it was very bare and miserable, compared with her usual homely jumble. I remember there was that transparent despair and it was very transparent and rather frightening. She kept up her standards by telling me that she had a dozen big projects in hand, but with all this bareness and the signs of poverty, it was obvious to me that she was beseiged.[57]

It was indeed ironic that as Ida became more and more desperate, and as her communication with the outside world became increasingly removed from reality, the photographic revival, which she had anticipated and indeed had prompted by her Whitechapel exhibition, had finally begun in Britain. Early in 1966, the photographer Jorge Lewinski wrote to invite her to exhibit in a planned biennial of British photography, to be mounted at the Festival Hall in 1967.[58] New and important photographic ventures within the medium were being initiated in London: a giant show of Cecil Beaton's photographs was mounted at the National Portrait Gallery in 1968. In that same year the first magazine for independent photographers, *Creative Camera*, was launched under the editorship of the innovative Bill Jay. In 1971, Sue Davies and Dorothy Bohm opened up the Photographers Gallery in an ornate former Lyons Corner House just off Leicester Square. In less than a decade, photography had progressed from being a shunned interloper to the most fashionable of the visual arts.

As public excitement about the medium grew, and interest in photographic publishing, collecting and exhibiting increased, Ida retreated into the shadows. By the beginning of the 1970s, she was sixty-two years old. She had achieved more recognition and more attention than any other post-war photographer in Britain. She had remained totally committed to her own notions of photographic excellence. She had produced portraiture which was not only compelling and skilful, but which formed a document of the post-war years quite unique in its scope and its intention. By 1970, she was almost forgotten. In her shabby bedsitter, she lived surrounded by her boxes of negatives, which she had carefully labelled with

Eugène Ionesco, dramatist, 1960

what she estimated to be their worth (one was marked 'very special negatives, worth £50,000'), and by the memory of a life spent in the pursuit of a photographic perfection.

Looking back now through her negative files, and through the prints she made during the hectic years at D'Arblay Street, her work still has the capacity to astonish, with its range of deep tones and its remarkable clarity. The quality of her work, the wit and acuteness of her vision, is still outstanding. On 24 December 1974, as Britain settled down for the Christmas festivities, Ida suffered a thrombosis and died alone in her Bayswater bedsitter. For several days, her absence went entirely unnoticed. Her funeral, held at the crematorium at Golders Green, was a quiet affair, with only a handful of mourners, including Robert Lassam and Mark Gerson. The funeral service was conducted by an Armenian priest from Ida's own church. To those who had first met Ida just after the war as a vibrant, energetic and outspoken photographer, who had seen her attack the barriers which the establishment had erected against the medium, who had shared her delight in her huge success at the Whitechapel, her sudden death seemed to be almost an impossibility. For Mark Gerson, who had made his way up the rickety stairs at Litchfield Street to watch Ida's early portrait sessions, it had seemed as if she was 'indestructible . . . I never thought she was going to die, she was one of those people who was ageless.'[59] For Josef Herman, who had made many drawings of Ida during the fifties, and who remembered her as one of his most exciting models as well as a great photographer and a good friend, 'When she died, it left a vacuum that no one else could fill. No one else could take her place. She was a complete original.'[60]

Ida Kar is one of the most important figures in our contemporary photographic history. More than any other individual, she was responsible for the public acceptance of the medium as an art in the early 1960s. Her exhibitions, in this country and abroad, attracted many thousands of visitors drawn from all walks of life. Her work was accessible, compellingly presented and dramatic. Her archive of photographs repays close study, for it is a document of her times quite unique in its intentions and its achievements. Ida Kar looked at the fifties with a gaze which was unblurred by notions of class or status or nationality. Her insistence on her status as an independent artist-photographer marked a new departure in the medium, and her pioneering exhibitions made the emergence of a modern photographic criticism inevitable. Her tragedy was perhaps that her work, seen at the beginning of the decade as highly innovative, was too swiftly superseded by the new pop portraiture of the 1960s. It

The portrayer and the portrayed: posing for the Armenian painter Sarian, 1962

Threne
for Ida

She has gone, and she will not return.
Each room is silent with her traces.
I have burned the photographs
And destroyed the jars
From which she would anoint herself
In secret places.

Hers was a life of humdrum ritual
Spent in the market and before the sink.
How could I know it was an honour
And not a trial,
Always to know, too soon,
What she would think?

Victor Musgrave *c.*1975

was tragic too that the strength of personality which so distinguished her, eventually became seen as truculence and eccentricity. Perhaps if she had been a man, her aggression would have been seen as determination, her egoism as sureness of purpose, but perhaps equally, if she had been a man, then she would not have felt that she need be so aggressive, or so egotistical. Ida became almost fanatically anxious for fame, perhaps because it seemed to validate her very existence. In the end, her status, real or imagined, as Britain's most famous photographer, became more important to her than photography itself. In her desperate search for celebrity through art, the process of the catharsis was forgotten, and only the display remained.

Looking through Ida's press cuttings books, reading her letters and speaking with her friends and colleagues, one is intensely aware of her vitality and her enormous presence. Lecturing, photographing, admonishing, gesticulating, advising and posing, cooking or singing, she always seemed to have some definite purpose, some particular end in view. Ida was remarkable in that she knew so little of reticence or modesty, that she believed in herself and her abilities so wholly. She stands out too for her honesty and her innocence, for her astonishing energy and for her never-failing receptivity to fresh ideas and new people.

London in the fifties was full of 'characters', men and women who, in the end, can be defined by their own eccentricity or outrageousness rather than for any real contribution to art or culture. Ida Kar was far more than that. In her photography she penetrated the thick skin of British artistic and literary life in the fifties and showed, with precision and wit, the vanities and preoccupations, the fantasies and the obsessions that lay beneath its surface. She provided a visual document of a cultural elite which is unique in its assertiveness, its perspicacity and its radical intent.

Metropolitan Music Hall, Edgware Road, London, mid-1950s

Metropolitan Music Hall, Edgware Road, London, mid-1950s

From a series on London pubs, mid-1950s

From a series on London pubs, mid-1950s

A shopkeeper in the Royal Opera Arcade, London, mid-1950s

A shopkeeper in the Royal Opera Arcade, London, mid-1950s

Street photograph, Soho, early 1950s

Street photograph, Soho, early 1950s

Cuba, 1964

Cuba, 1964

Sir Jacob Epstein, sculptor, London, 1953

Bertrand Russell, London, 1952

John Christoforou, painter, London, 1953

Francis Newton Souza, painter, London, mid-1950s

Stanley William Hayter, artist, 1960

Josef Herman, painter, London, 1960

Patrick Heron, painter and writer, 1954

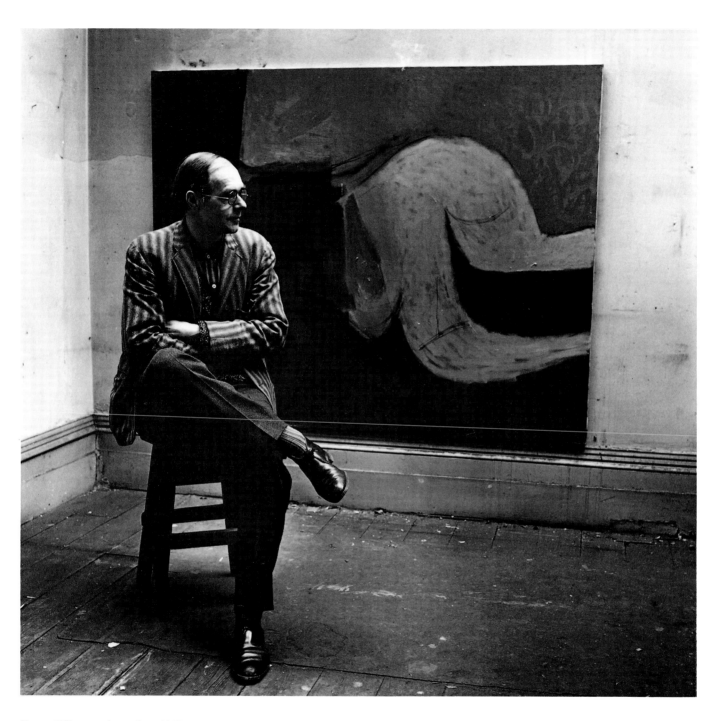

Roger Hilton, painter, late 1950s

Iris Murdoch, writer, late 1950s

Penelope Mortimer, writer, London, 1961

Ronald Duncan, writer, 1951

Jacques Clementi, painter, Paris, early 1950s

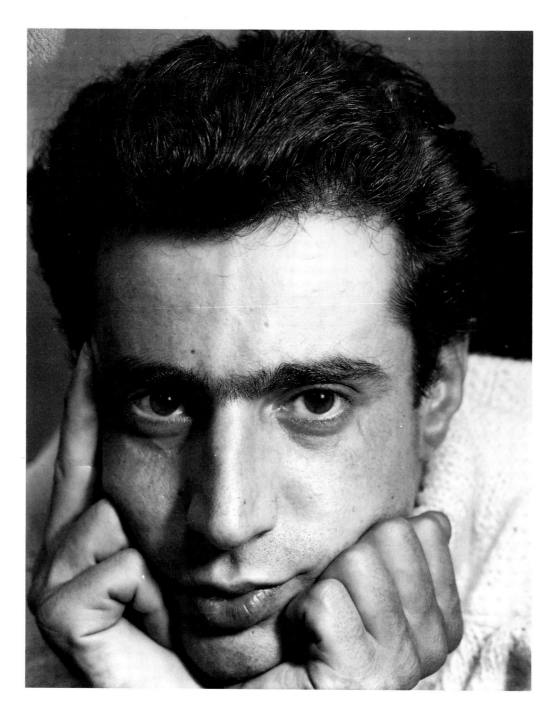

Tom Maschler, editor, London, mid-1950s

William Scott, painter, London, 1954

Alexander Weatherson, sculptor, London, 1959

Lynn Chadwick, sculptor, 1954

T. S. Eliot, poet and writer, London, 1956

Somerset Maugham posing for a head by Jacob Epstein, mid-1950s

Bill Hopkins, writer, London, early 1950s

Colin MacInnes, writer, 1960

F. E. McWilliam, sculptor, London, mid-1950s

Eduardo Paolozzi, sculptor, 1959

Stephen Spender, poet and critic, 1957

Laura del Rivo, writer, London, mid-1950s

Camille Bombois, painter, France, 1954

Fernand Léger, artist, France, 1954

Man Ray, artist, 1954

Georges Braque, painter, France, 1960

Olivia Manning, writer, London, 1960

Maggie Smith, actor, London, c. 1960

Erica Brausen, gallery director, London, 1959

Sir John Rothenstein in the sculpture hall at the Tate Gallery, London, 1960

Craigie Aitchison, painter, London, 1957

John Piper, painter, 1954

Laurie Lee, writer, late 1950s

Brendan Behan, writer, London, 1959

Jean Cocteau, France, early 1950s

Marc Chagall, painter, France, 1954

Elisabeth Frink, sculptor, 1956

Kenneth Armitage, sculptor, 1954

Sandra Blow, painter, London, 1955

Bryan Robertson, gallery director, London, 1958

Cecil Beaton, photographer and designer, Wiltshire, 1960

André Breton, writer, and his wife, Elisa, 1960

Barbara Hepworth, sculptor, 1954

Henry Moore at his studio in Much Hadham, 1954

Doris Lessing, writer, late 1950s

Dmitri Shostakovitch, composer, 1959

Joyce Cary, writer, Oxford, 1956

John Lehmann, writer and editor, London, late 1950s

Jack Smith, painter, London, 1959

Brian and Susan Robbins at the Farm Coffee Bar, London, 1960

Graham Sutherland, painter, 1954

Stanley Spencer, painter, 1954

William Turnbull, sculptor, 1955

Keith Vaughan, painter, 1960

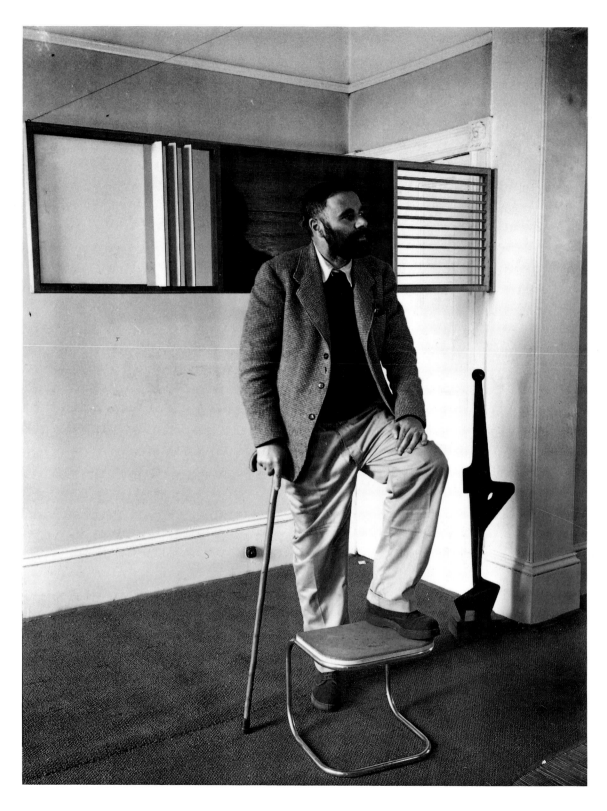

Victor Pasmore, artist, 1954

Reg Butler, sculptor, 1954

Marie-Hélène Vieira de Silva, artist, 1960

Enrico Baj, painter, 1956

Ivon Hitchens, painter, Sussex, 1954

Martin Bradley, artist, London, c. 1955

Alberto Giacometti, sculptor, France, 1954

Gino Severini, artist, mid-1950s

Nicolai Tomsky, sculptor, Moscow, 1959

Le Corbusier, architect and painter, France, 1954

Tsugouharu Foujita, artist, France, 1954

John Bratby, painter, 1959

Shelagh Delaney, writer, London, 1959

Eugène Ionesco, dramatist, 1960

Ida Kar made many hundreds of photographic portraits from 1950 to 1962. The following are most of her well-known and distinguished sitters.

Konrad Adenauer
Larry Adler
Craigie Aitchison
Kingsley Amis
Pietro Annigoni and pupils
Karel Appell
Kenneth Armitage
Jean Arp
Gillian Ayres
Enrico Baj
Jean Bazaine
Cecil Beaton
Brendan Behan
Sandra Blow
Camille Bombois
Martin Bradley
John Bratby
Georges Braque
Erica Brausen
Brassai
André Breton
Boris Brunov
Reg Butler
Chan Canasta
Massimo Campigli
Joyce Cary
Fidel Castro
Blaise Cendrars
Marc Chagall
Raymond Chandler
John Christoforou
Randolph Churchill
Le Corbusier
Jacques Clementi
Jean Cocteau
Noel Coward
Alan Davie
Shelagh Delaney
George Devine
Jane Drew and Maxwell Fry
Jean Dubuffet
Ronald Duncan
Alan Dunn
Ilya Ehrenburg

T. S. Eliot
Jacob Epstein
Margot Fonteyn
Christina Foyle
Lady Antonia Fraser
Dame Elisabeth Frink
Terry Frost
Tsugouharu Foujita
Billy Fury
William Gear
Helmut Gernsheim
Alberto Giacometti
Penelope Gilliatt
Ram Gopal
Marcel Gromaire
Peggy Guggenheim
Pamela Hansford Johnson
Norman Hartnell
Hans Hartung
Jacquetta Hawkes
Patrick Hayman
Stanley Hayter
Michael Heard
Adrian Heath
Dame Barbara Hepworth
Josef Herman
Patrick Heron
Anthony Hill
Roger Hilton
Ivon Hitchens
Bill Hopkins
Aldous Huxley
Eugene Ionesco
Avetik Isahakian
John Kasmin
Arthur Koestler
Yves Klein
David de Keyser
Bernard Kops
Peter Lanyon
John Latham
Marie Laurencin
Jenny Lee
Laurie Lee

Bernard Leach
Fernand Léger
Madame Léger
John Lehmann
Doris Lessing
C. Day Lewis
Gina Lollobrigida
L. S. Lowry
Sir Compton MacKenzie
Colin MacInnes
F. E. McWilliam
Olivia Manning
Moshe Maurer
Somerset Maugham
Bernard Meadows
E. L. T. Mesens
Sergio Mikoyan
Henry Miller
John Milne
Joan Miró
Denis Mitchell
Dudley Moore
Henry Moore
Alan Moorhead
Alberto Moravia
Penelope Mortimer
Iris Murdoch
Victor Musgrave
Anna Neagle
Sidney Nolan
Frank Norman
Eduardo Paolozzi
Victor Pasmore
Roland Penrose
John Piper
John Pope-Hennessy
J. B. Priestley
Anna Quayle
Man Ray
Laura del Rivo
Ceri Richards
Germaine Richier
Bridget Riley

Brian Robbins
Susan Robbins
Bryan Robertson
Sir John Rothenstein
Lord Bertrand Russell
William Saroyan
Jean-Paul Sartre
William Scott
Gino Severini
Ben Shahn
Dmitri Shostakovitch
Ann Sharpley
Marie-Hélène Vieira da Silva
Jack Smith
Maggie Smith
C. P. Snow
Yolanda Sonnabend
Pierre Soulages
F. N. Souza
Stanley Spencer
Stephen Spender
Graham Sutherland
David Sylvester
Angela Thirkell
Franchot Tone
Dudley Tooth
Kenneth Tynan
Feliks Topolski
Julian Trevelyan
William Turnbull
Laurens Van Der Post
Keith Vaughan
Jacques Villon
John Wain
Alex Weatherston
Sir Charles Wheeler
Tennessee Williams
Colin Wilson
Scottie Wilson
Bryan Wynter
Monica Wynter
Osip Zadkine
Mai Zetterling

N O T E S

INTRODUCTION
Pictures of the lost decade
An introduction to Ida Kar's photography

1. From the introduction by Franz Roh to *L. Moholy Nagy: 60 photos*. Published by Klinkhardt and Biermann, Berlin, 1930.
2. From *The Angry Decade*, by N. Kenneth Allsop. Published by Peter Owen, 1958, p. 40.

CHAPTER ONE
Becoming Idabel
From Armenia to Alexandria 1908–1945

1. From Evelyn Waugh's *When the Going Was Good*. Published London, 1948.
2. From an unpublished typescript, written by Heinrich Heidersberger in 1989. Translated from the German by Dorothy Bohm, February 1989.
3. *Ibid.*
4. *Ibid.*
5. *Ibid.*
6. *Ibid.*
7. *Ibid.*
8. *Ibid.*
9. From a letter from Ida Kar to Heinrich Heidersberger, 9 August 1934. Translated from the French by Amanda Hopkinson, September 1988. Heinrich Heidersberger papers.
10. From a review of the Whitechapel exhibition written by Jasia Reichardt in *Arts News and Review*, 26 March 1960.
11. Unpublished typescript written by Victor Musgrave, n.d. Lent to the author by Dorothy Bohm.
12. From the *British Journal of Photography*, 16 March 1962.
13. Unpublished typescript written by Victor Musgrave, n.d. Lent by Dorothy Bohm.

CHAPTER TWO
I looked in from the outside and what did I see?
Photographing bohemia in the 1950s

1. Cyril Connolly writing in *Horizon*, 1949.
2. Bill Hopkins in conversation with the author, September 1988.
3. Mark Gerson in conversation with the author, February 1988.
4. *Ibid.*
5. *Ibid.*
6. *Ibid.*
7. *Ibid.*
8. John Kasmin in conversation with the author, November 1988.
9. Josef Herman in conversation with the author, March 1988.
10. *Ibid.*
11. *Ibid.*
12. From the *Listener*, n.d. (Ida Kar papers).
13. Bill Hopkins in conversation with the author, September 1988.
14. *Ibid.*
15. F. N. Souza in a letter to the author, 28 September 1988.
16. Bill Hopkins in conversation with the author, September 1988.
17. *Ibid.*
18. F. N. Souza in a letter to the author, 28 September 1988.
19. Bill Hopkins in conversation with the author, September 1988.
20. From a telephone conversation between the author and William Scott's son, November 1988.
21. Information from Mark Gerson, February 1988.
22. Jack Smith in a letter to the author, September 1988.
23. Sandra Blow in a letter to the author, 10 February 1988.
24. Bridget Riley in a letter to the author, 6 October 1988.
25. William Gear in a letter to the author, 27 January 1988.
26. F. N. Souza in a letter to the author, 28 September 1988.
27. John Kasmin in conversation with the author, November 1988.
28. This, previous and subsequent comments by John Kasmin all quoted from *ibid.*
29. *Ibid.*
30. Ida Kar in a letter to Victor Musgrave, 10 August 1957. Ida Kar papers.
31. *Ibid.*
32. *Ibid.*
33. *Ibid.*
34. Ida Kar in a letter to Victor Musgrave, 23 August 1957. Ida Kar papers.
35. *Ibid.*
36. *Ibid.*
37. *Ibid.*
38. Ida Kar to Victor Musgrave, 1 September 1957. Ida Kar papers.
39. *Ibid.*
40. *Ibid.*
41. *Ibid.*
42. Cecil Beaton in a letter to Ida Kar, *c*. 1959. Ida Kar papers.
43. Josef Herman in conversation with the author, March 1988.
44. From a letter from Ida Kar to Victor Musgrave, n.d. Ida Kar papers.

CHAPTER THREE
In this purblind land
Photography in the 1950s and the Whitechapel exhibition

1. Cecil Beaton, *The Strenuous Years 1948–53*, Weidenfeld and Nicolson, 1973, pp. 2–3.
2. Godfrey Thurston Hopkins in conversation with the author in 1988.

#30
= L.M